grow it, cook it
with kids

grow it, cook it
with kids

Amanda Grant

photography by Tara Fisher

RYLAND
PETERS
& SMALL

LONDON NEW YORK

For Ella, Lola, Finley, Liliana & Saskia –
keep planting and cooking!

Senior Designer Iona Hoyle
Senior Editor Céline Hughes
Location Researcher Jess Walton
Head of Production Patricia Harrington
Art Director Leslie Harrington
Publishing Director Alison Starling

Prop and Food Stylist Amanda Grant
Photoshoot Assistant Brenda Bishop
Gardening Consultant and Indexer
Richard Bird

First published in the UK in 2010
by Ryland Peters & Small
20–21 Jockey's Fields
London WC1R 4BW
www.rylandpeters.com

10 9 8 7 6 5 4 3 2 1

Text © Amanda Grant 2010
Design and photographs
© Ryland Peters & Small 2010

ISBN: 978-1-84597-968-3

A CIP record for this book is available
from the British Library.

Printed in China

Notes

• All spoon measurements are level unless
otherwise specified.

• Ovens should be preheated to the
specified temperatures. All ovens work
slightly differently. We recommend using an
oven thermometer and suggest you consult
the maker's handbook for any special
instructions, particularly if you are cooking
in a fan-assisted oven, as you will need to
adjust temperatures according to
manufacturer's instructions.

• All eggs are medium, unless otherwise
specified. It is recommended that free-range
eggs be used.

• Recipes containing raw or partially
cooked egg, or raw fish or shellfish, should
not be served to the very young, very old,
anyone with a compromised immune
system or pregnant women.

Neither the author nor the publisher can be
held responsible for any claim arising out
of the information in this book. Always
consult your health advisor or doctor if
you have any concerns about your child's
health or nutrition.

contents

introduction

When you start to grow your own vegetables you learn about the life cycles of the vegetables, the creatures attracted to the garden, the soil, nutrition and science.

You will also learn about seasonality, which means at which time of year the fruits and vegetables are ready to eat. This is why gardening and cooking go hand in hand.

Growing a few of your favourite fruits and vegetables can be really exciting and rewarding, but you also need to know what to do with your fruits and vegetables in the kitchen so that you can enjoy eating them.

This book will show you how to sow seeds and plant small plants, how to look after the plants so that they are healthy and grow well, how to pick your crop (the fruits and vegetables) and then how to prepare and cook them in the kitchen so that you and your family can enjoy delicious home-grown meals.

Each chapter is divided into sections so that you can easily follow each stage – they are called Plant It, Grow It, Pick It, 5 Ways (quick ways to use the fruit or vegetable) and Cook It, where you will find a selection of easy recipes.

Once you have grown a tub of potatoes, for example, you then need to know how to clean or peel them and how to boil or steam them so that you can eat them for supper.

Similarly, when strawberries are ripe and ready to eat you will need to learn how to hull the fruit (to take off the green stalk) and then how to cut them into quarters so that you can enjoy them with a scoop of ice cream. These skills are basic kitchen skills that you will find really useful throughout your life.

Sometimes you will need **an adult to help you** in the garden or in the kitchen, for example to cut back big plants or make holes in plant pots, or when taking hot dishes out of the oven or using a food processor.

When you have learnt some new skills, practised them and grown in confidence, you will soon be able to start doing things by yourself, and maybe even cook a whole meal using some of your home-grown produce!

gardening basics

Plants are living things, just like you! There are three important things that plants need: water, food and sunlight. If you prepare the soil well, plants can make their own food. They will gather sunlight on their leaves and use it to change water and air into food to give them lots of energy for growing. Clever things!

Your own patch!

To prepare the soil for planting, here's what you'll need to do:

• If possible, ask your parents to have your own space in the garden.

• Make sure you choose a sunny spot that is sheltered from the wind.

• Pull all the weeds out of the soil. It makes it easier to keep the weeds under control later on.

• Spread a layer of well-rotted manure or home-made compost over the soil and then have fun digging it into your patch. This is really important to give plants extra nutrients and a bit more energy. You can buy well-rotted manure from farms or stables, or make your own compost by keeping a compost heap. It might be a bit smelly, but the plants will love it!

Making a raised bed

A raised bed makes weeding much easier and you don't need to stand on the soil, which would normally squash it. To make a raised bed, you will need wooden planks to make a square frame. Their size depends on the space you have, but a good size is about 2 metres by 1 metre. You can raise it as high as you like, but about 15 cm should be your minimum. Top the bed up with soil and good compost.

What is compost?

Compost is made from plant and vegetable waste left over in the kitchen. When it rots, it makes a dark, crumbly substance which is nutritious to plants.

'Compost' just means a 'mixture', so all kinds of things can go in – carrot and potato peelings, and pea and bean pods, and even teabags, crushed-up eggshells and lawn mowings from the garden (see middle picture on the page opposite). Don't use cooked food and meat, though, as it might attract pests.

Making a compost heap

A compost heap can simply be 'a heap' but using or making a container will make your heap tidier. The size of your heap will depend on your garden – remember you might have a lot to put on it but when the compost rots down it takes up less room.

If you decide to make a container, **an adult will need to help you**, as you will have to use wood, metal or plastic to make a box. When you start putting your kitchen waste in, cover it with some polythene or cardboard to speed up the rotting.

Pot plants

If you're growing plants in pots, you need

something better than normal garden soil to protect the plants and seeds from pests and give them a healthy start. Use a general-purpose or potting compost that comes in bags from garden centres.

You'll need to be especially careful to water pot plants so they don't dry out. To make sure the water doesn't get stuck in the pot, put some stones or broken terracotta in the bottom of the pot so water can drain away.

Garden tools

It's fun to have your own gardening tools. You won't need too many:

Fork: For weeding and getting rid of lumps in the soil, and for mixing in your compost. If you grow root vegetables like potatoes, use it to raise them carefully from the soil. Be very careful of its sharp prongs.

Spade: For digging or loosening the soil, or to move compost from your heap to your garden beds.

Trowel: Like a spade but will help you get in all the nooks and crannies that a spade is too big for. You'll need it for potting plants and sowing seeds.

Rake: For breaking up small lumps in the soil and preparing it for sowing seeds. It can also be used to help scrape up fallen leaves in the autumn.

Watering can: For giving plants the water they need. You'll have to use it every day in the hot summer months.

Pests

Unfortunately you're not the only one that wants to taste your delicious garden produce. Watch out for snails and caterpillars, especially on green vegetables like cabbages and lettuces, slugs in potatoes, and wasps in fruit.

Be on the lookout for pests all the time. If you have lots of them, look for organic ways to get rid of them in your local garden centre.

More handy gardening tips

Netting: If you need netting to protect soft fruits, choose thick netting. Birds' feet can sometimes get caught in very fine net and then cats and other predators can get to the trapped birds.

Weather: A good gardener should always think about the weather. For example, if it's very dry and hot your plants will need more water.

Planting: Different seeds must be planted at different times of the year. Make sure to read the back of seed packets to check you're planting them at the right time.

Rotating: Try not to plant potatoes, onions, and tomatoes in the same part of the garden each year. This is called 'rotating crops' and farmers do it to make sure their soil stays healthy.

Companion planting

Sometimes plants are happier when they are near another type of plant. Some plants can help other plants by providing the right nutrients, offering protection from the sun or wind or stopping pests from eating the plants. For example, marigolds can help keep bugs away from tomatoes.

cooking basics

The great thing with cooking is that you can have fun in the kitchen and at the same time make delicious food for your family and friends to eat. You will also be learning some great skills throughout this book, skills that you will use for the rest of your life.

Before you begin

You need to remember a few things that will help make sure there are no accidents and that you don't hurt either yourself or anyone else who is cooking with you.

Always **ask an adult** before you start to make sure that they are happy that you are cooking and check that they will be around to help if you need it.

Wear an apron to help keep the dirt from your clothes falling into the food that you are making.

Wash your hands before you begin and dry them on a clean towel.

Always wear oven gloves when you put food into the oven or take it out and **ask an adult to help you** with the oven, hob (top of the oven) and grill.

Kitchen utensils

You don't need lots of equipment to have fun cooking, but it helps to have a few basic things like:

Wooden spoon: For all that mixing.

Whisk: For whipping, e.g. whipping cream for a Strawberry Eton Mess (see page 114).

Rolling pin: For rolling out pastry (and sometimes bashing!).

Weighing scales: What's great about cooking is that you can practise things that you are learning at school – like maths – when you measure and weigh out ingredients.

Small, sharp knife: Once you know how to hold your knife properly and to cut, there are so many things that you can make to eat. The two main cutting techniques are the 'bridge' and the 'claw' techniques (see below). Once you have learnt how to master these you can cut most things safely.

Other useful utensils: A grater, a vegetable peeler, a garlic crusher, a cake tin, baking tray, roasting tin and a few saucepans can come in handy, too.

'Bridge' cutting technique

Hold the item by forming a bridge with your thumb on one side of the food and your index finger on the other side. Hold the knife in your other hand with the blade facing down and guide the knife under the bridge and cut through the food. For some soft items, such as tomatoes, it might be easier to puncture the tomato skin with the point of the knife before cutting.

'Claw' cutting technique

Place the flat side of the item down on the chopping board. Shape the fingers of the left hand into a claw shape, tucking the thumb inside the fingers. Rest the claw on the item to be sliced. Holding the knife in the right hand slice the item, moving the 'clawed' fingers away as cutting progresses.

You will see these techniques being used throughout the book. Look at the section on '5 Ways with..' in each chapter for instructions on how to chop and slice individual vegetables and fruit.

Cracking eggs

Hold the egg in one hand – in fact cup it in your hand so that it is nice and secure. Hold it over a small bowl. Take a table knife in your other hand and hit the middle of the egg with the knife to crack it (see picture on opposite page, top left).

Put the knife down and then put your thumbs into the slit and pull the shell apart (see picture on opposite page, top right).

Let the egg drop into the bowl (see picture on opposite page, bottom left). Your eggs are now ready to use.

A recipe might ask you to lightly beat them before using them. Using a fork, lightly beat them so that the egg yolks and whites are evenly mixed.

Creaming butter and sugar

Many cake and biscuit recipes start with beating sugar and butter together until they are well mixed and they have become pale and fluffy. This method is called 'creaming' and it's very important as it gives a lighter texture to cakes or biscuits. There are a few things to remember before you begin: butter gives a much better flavour than margarine; cakes and biscuits are best made with unsalted butter; and always leave the butter out of the fridge for at least half an hour before you begin so that it is soft enough to beat.

herbs & leaves

planting herbs

If you want to have a go at growing some fresh herbs, you might like to start with some of these – rosemary, thyme, sage, mint, parsley and basil.

Rosemary, thyme, sage, mint, parsley and basil are all useful in the kitchen and are easy to grow from 'plug plants' (see Glossary, page 122) or small plants. Have a look in a garden centre or greengrocer for small pots of herbs. Spend time choosing your herbs – smell and if possible, taste them first. Then you need to choose whether to grow them in a pot or directly in the garden soil. Mint needs special treatment, so check the page opposite for this.

Planting in pots

Ideally about 2 hours before you start the gardening, water your plant in its pot.

1 PICK A POT

Choose pots with holes in the bottom – herbs don't like getting their feet wet so the water needs to be able to drain out. Put some broken pots, shells or small stones in the bottom of the pots.

2 ADD SOIL

Three-quarters fill the pot with a general-purpose potting compost and use your trowel to dig a little hole in the centre of the compost for the plant.

3 TIP THE PLANT OUT

Carefully tip the plant out of the pot and try to keep as much compost around the roots as possible. Put the plant into the hole with its roots facing down.

4 TUCK THE PLANT IN

Fill in more soil around the plant, gently press it down with your hands, then give it a good drink of water.

Planting in the garden

Ideally about 2 hours before you start the gardening, water your plant in its pot.

1 PREPARE THE SOIL

Rake the top of the soil to break up any lumps. Spread a layer of well-rotted manure or your own compost over the soil and have fun digging it into the soil.

2 DIG A HOLE

Dig a hole with your trowel in the soil.

3 TIP THE PLANT OUT

Carefully tip the plant out of the pot and try to keep as much compost around the roots as possible. Put the plant into the hole with its roots facing down.

4 TUCK THE PLANT IN

Fill in more soil around the plant, gently press it down with your hands, then give it a good drink of water. These herbs don't need much food but they are happier in soil that drains water well – see page 18 for how to look after them.

If you want to grow herbs from seed, look at the instructions for leaves on page 17.

How to plant mint

You have to watch mint – it needs to be kept in a pot otherwise its roots can take over the garden! But if you want to plant it in the ground you can always do what my granny taught me to do. Find an old bucket or plastic plant pot and **ask an adult** to cut out its bottom so that it has sides but no base. Dig a big hole in the soil – big enough for your pot – then put the pot into the hole. Put the mint inside the pot and fill with soil around the mint. It can grow but its roots will stay in one place.

planting leaves & radishes

Choose your leaves

There are so many salad leaves to choose from, including rocket, cut-and-come-again and lettuce, that the first thing you need to do is decide which you'd like to grow and eat. They vary a lot in flavour.

Sowing in the garden

If you want to sow your seeds outside in the ground, you will need warm weather, which should be around early spring.

1 PREPARE THE SOIL

Rake the top of the soil to break up any lumps. Spread a layer of well-rotted manure or your own compost over the soil and have fun digging it into the soil. Water the soil.

2 DIG A HOLE

If you want your leaves to grow in a neat line, you need to mark out a row to sow along. Put sticks at each end of the row and tie string to the sticks. Drag a trowel along the soil under the string to make a small furrow 1 cm deep.

3 SOW THE SEEDS

For 'cut-and-come-again' leaves (see Glossary, page 122) you can sow 6–8 seeds together then leave a gap of 10 cm before you sow the next 6–8 seeds. For other leaves and radishes, sow the seeds in a single, continuous line along the furrow. Cover with the soil and press down.

4 WATER THE SEEDS

Water the seeds with a special watering can that just sprinkles water gently – if you pour too much water onto the soil in a big gush it might wash the seeds away!

5 SOW MORE SEEDS

Keep the rest of the seeds in the packet and after 2 weeks, if you have the space in your garden, you could sow another patch of seeds in exactly the same way. This way the leaves will be ready at different stages through the summer. You should see some green shoots popping up in a week's time.

Sowing inside

If you don't have much room in your garden or you want to sow some leaves slightly earlier in the year, then you can have a go at sowing them inside. A small plant tray or an old ice cream tub will do – **ask an adult** to make holes in the bottom so that your seeds don't become waterlogged! Put some broken pots, shells or small stones in the bottom of the pots.

Three-quarters fill the tray with a general-purpose potting compost. Sow the seeds 1–1.5 cm deep and 3 cm apart. Cover with a little more compost. Water well.

When the shoots are about 5 cm tall, if you are growing rocket or cut-and-come-again, you can either continue to grow them in your tray, or transfer them into the garden or into a bigger pot. For lettuces, you will always need to transfer them into the garden or into a bigger pot.

Planting in the garden

1 PREPARE THE SOIL

Rake the top of the soil to break up any lumps. Spread a layer of well-rotted

manure or your own compost over the soil and have fun digging it into the soil.

2 DIG A HOLE

Dig a hole with your trowel in the soil.

3 TIP THE PLANT OUT

Carefully take the seedling out of the tray – poke a pencil into the soil near the seedling and gently ease the seedling out without damaging the roots. Put the plant into the hole with its roots facing down.

4 TUCK THE PLANT IN

Fill in more soil around the plant, gently press it down with your hands, then give it a good drink of water. Plant the seedlings 10 cm apart.

Planting in pots

Choose pots with holes in the bottom. Three-quarters fill the pots with a general-purpose potting compost.

Cover with a thin layer of compost and gently press down with the back of your hand or hoe and water. Then you can move the pot to a sunny, sheltered spot.

growing herbs & leaves

Growing herbs

Herbs tend to be very easy to grow and don't need too much looking after.

Herbs growing in pots should be kept in a spot where they are out of the midday sun and you need to make sure that they don't dry out fully. However, they don't like to be wet either! So the only way to keep them healthy is to keep an eye on them. If the plant is showing signs of wilting you are letting them get too dry.

In their first year herbs may need more regular watering if it is particularly hot and dry. Just keep your eye on them – if they are growing well and look healthy, then you are looking after them well.

Weed around the herbs through the spring, summer and autumn. In the autumn, spread a layer of compost or your own well-rotted manure, about 5–10 cm thick, around the plants.

Winter is the time for herbs to rest. Pull up any weeds and rake the soil, then wait for spring to arrive!

If you have planted herbs in window boxes you will need to check on make sure they always have enough water.

Growing sage

You will need to **ask an adult** to prune your sage bush in the spring to prevent it from going woody. If you don't look after it you may find that the plant flops open in the middle and the central thick woody stems won't produce new leaves.

Flowering

As soon as herbs have flowered, cut their flowers off. Try sprinkling chive flowers over salads (see page 121). Chives can be cut back to about 5 cm off the ground after they have flowered (see picture, below centre) – they will grow back again.

Some herbs like basil and chives will only survive during the summer.

Salad leaves

Salad leaves are pretty easy to grow and don't need much looking after, but you do need to be aware of a few things.

Salad leaves do need to drink – you must keep the plants watered – but try not to over-water them. Check them as often as you can and just water them when they are looking slightly dry.

As you see the leaves growing, start to 'thin' by picking some of them along the line to leave space for the other leaves to grow. Keep an eye on the leaves – they will need to be harvested (picked) regularly and if you see any with holes in them or any that are looking brown or not as fresh as the others, pick them and put them on the compost heap.

If you're growing rocket and it starts to flower, pick the flower buds and their stems off the plant and put them on the compost. This will mean that the plant will keep producing tasty leaves for longer.

harvesting & preparing herbs & leaves

This is so exciting! Now that you have grown fresh herbs you will be able to pick and use them whenever you need them! It is also so much cheaper than buying fresh herbs from the shops. I hope you have fun using them in the recipes.

With the bushy 'perennial' herbs (see Glossary, page 122) like rosemary, thyme and sage that are available all year round, you will need to use scissors to cut the stalks from the plant. Always **ask an adult to help you** with this.

Chives

Cut the chives at the bottom of the stem – 3 cm above the ground – so that the plant continues to grow. If a stem is flowering, cut it and throw away the stem, but pull apart the flower (see picture on page 18, below centre) and sprinkle it onto a salad.

Basil and parsley

Keep picking both of these herbs through the summer. With basil (see picture opposite, bottom), pinch out the tops to keep the plant producing new growth. With parsley, pick the large outside stems. Only pick the middle stem if it is flowering.

Storing herbs

It is best to leave herbs in their pots or flower beds and just pick them when you need them. But if you have picked more herbs than you need, there are a few ways that you can keep them and use them later.

Put the harvested herbs into a small bag to keep in the salad tray in the fridge. They should last for up to 10 days.

See Way 1, on the next page, about freezing herbs. When you want to add some fresh herbs to your cooking, you can just add an ice cube of herbs!

Cut-and-come-again salad leaves & spinach

After 4–6 weeks, when the leaves are about 5–8 cm long, they will be ready to pick. Before you pick the salad leaves it is a good idea to give the plants a really good water so that they are fresh and crisp when you pick them.

When you are picking your cut-and-come-again leaves you need to leave about 2–3 cm of the plant behind. This way the plant can start to grow again. They should grow four or five times before they stop growing any more. If you have sown some seeds at different intervals (with a few weeks in between each) then you should have cut-and-come-again leaves all through the summer.

It is also a good idea to pick leaves from different plants and leave some leaves behind too. For example, if the plant has 10 leaves, pick 5 of the leaves and leave 5. In a few days or the following week you can pick the 5 that you left behind. This gives the plant a chance to grow strong and stay healthy.

You will need to give the leaves a good wash and shake them to dry them a little or rest them on kitchen paper, cover them with kitchen paper and just press them lightly to dry slightly.

Radishes

Radishes grow quickly – after 4 weeks, pull one out of the ground to see if it is ready to eat. If they get too big they can become slightly woody in texture and not quite as tasty. Pick every other radish to leave space for the ones left to grow.

Wash them in a bowl of cold water. Cut the leaves off and trim the root end using the 'claw' cutting technique (see page 11).

Give them a quick wash, take off their leaves, wrap them in kitchen paper and keep them in the fridge for a few days.

5 ways with herbs & leaves

Herbs have been grown for thousands of years. They are used to add flavour and a scent (smell) to food. Some herbs are also used to make medicines and perfumes. The herbs' flavour and scent come from oils found inside the leaves. If you pick a herb leaf and crush it between your fingers you will squeeze the oil out of the leaf and then be able to smell the herb. This is why we normally chop the herbs into small pieces before we cook with them to help release the oil into the food. If you have grown some salad leaves as well as herbs, have fun adding them to your sandwiches or make a lovely dressing to drizzle over the top before you eat them.

1 HERB ICE CUBES

If you have picked lots of fresh herbs and you can't use them all straightaway, you might like to freeze some for later. Pull the leaves off the stems and then using scissors, chop the leaves into small pieces. Divide the herbs between the holes of an ice cube tray and pour over water. Carefully put the tray into the freezer to freeze. Pop an ice cube of herbs out of the tray when you need it and add to a soup, pasta sauce or anything else that you are cooking!

2 MINT TEA

Ask an adult to help you make mint tea. Pick a handful of fresh mint leaves and put them into a teapot. Then you will need to ask an adult to boil the kettle and fill the teapot with boiling water. Leave for a few minutes. Ask an adult if you can pour the tea into cups to half-fill and then add cold water until it is cool enough to drink.

5 WAYS

3 HOME-GROWN SALAD WITH DRESSING

Have you ever made a vinaigrette salad dressing with oil and something acidic like lemon juice or vinegar? In a clean jam jar (with a lid) measure 1 tablespoon of red or white wine vinegar, balsamic vinegar or lemon juice with 3 tablespoons of good olive oil. Add a teaspoon of runny honey or a pinch of light soft brown sugar. Screw on the lid and give it a good shake. If you like garlic, crush ½ clove and add to the dressing. Pick some of your salad leaves, wash and put into a bowl. Drizzle with dressing.

4 WILTED SPINACH

Pick 4 or 5 BIG handfuls of spinach leaves. Wash the spinach in cold water and shake so that the leaves are clean but still slightly wet. Put them into a saucepan, put the lid on and put on the hob. **Ask an adult to help you** turn on the hob to high. Lift the lid and stir the spinach now and then with a wooden spoon. Cook until the leaves have all wilted – you will be amazed how much they shrivel up! Using oven gloves take the pan off the hob – you don't want to overcook the spinach.

5 RADISHES WITH CREAM CHEESE

You may need **an adult to help you** cut the radish. Hold a radish by its green leaves and rest on a chopping board. Using a small sharp knife cut a 'V' shape in the root end of the radish – making sure that you keep your fingers holding the green leaves well away from the knife. Using a teaspoon, spoon a little cream cheese into the 'V' and eat. The creamy flavour from the cheese works really well with the peppery radish.

big 'everything you have grown' salad with croutons

If you have had fun growing some salad leaves and tomatoes, now is the time to throw them together and enjoy eating them! If you haven't grown all of these things, you can still enjoy making and eating a salad.

1 To make the croutons, turn the oven on to 180°C (350°F) Gas 4.

2 Cut the slices of bread into small cubes using the 'claw' cutting technique (see page 11). Put the cubes into a roasting tin, sprinkle the oil over the top and use your hands to mix the bread around in the oil. Using your oven gloves, put the tin in the oven for 10 minutes.

3 Using oven gloves, take the tin out of the oven and mix the croutons with a wooden spoon. Put back into the oven for 10 minutes or until the croutons are golden and crunchy.

4 Meanwhile, to make the salad, slice the cucumber into thin slices using the 'claw' cutting technique and cut the tomatoes in half using the 'bridge' cutting technique (see page 11). Wash the spinach (or chard) and rocket and shake gently to get rid of a bit of the water. Put into a big salad bowl with the cucumber and tomatoes and any other home-grown salad leaves you'd like to add.

5 In a glass jar or small jug mix together the lemon juice and olive oil for the dressing and drizzle over the salad. Toss everything together with salad serving spoons.

6 Finally, drop in the lovely crispy croutons (add them at the last minute so they don't go soggy in the dressing!) and toss the salad again. Serve immediately.

COOK IT

ingredients

for the croutons

4 thick slices of brown or white bread

2 tablespoons olive oil

for the salad

½ cucumber

about 8 cherry tomatoes (of different colours if you have them)

4 handfuls of baby spinach (or chard) leaves

4 handfuls of rocket leaves

any more of your home-grown salad leaves

for the dressing

1 tablespoon lemon juice

3 tablespoons olive oil

makes enough for 4

green rice

This tastes amazing and looks a pretty green colour! Always **ask an adult to help you** with a food processor and remember that the blade in the middle of the processor is very sharp.

ingredients

1 green pepper

2 spring onions

a big bunch of mixed fresh herbs, e.g. parsley, chives, coriander

2 cloves of garlic

3 tablespoons olive oil

225 g basmati rice

600 ml chicken stock

makes enough for 4

COOK IT

1 Using the 'bridge' cutting technique (see page 11), cut the pepper in half and scoop out the seeds with your fingers. Using the 'bridge' cutting technique cut the pepper halves into big pieces and **ask an adult to help you** put them into a food processor.

2 Using the 'claw' cutting technique (see page 11), cut the ends off the spring onion. Peel off one layer of the onion if it looks battered or wrinkled. Using the 'bridge' cutting technique, cut into chunks and add to the processor.

3 Using scissors, snip off the ends of the herb stalks and put the herbs into a food processor. Peel the skin off the cloves of garlic and add to the processor.

4 Put the lid on the food processor and **ask an adult to help you** whiz everything together until you get quite a smooth green paste.

5 **Ask an adult to help you** heat the olive oil in a heavy-based saucepan.

6 Remove the lid from the food processor and spoon the paste into the saucepan. Cook gently, stirring every now and then with a wooden spoon, for about 5 minutes.

7 Add the rice and fry for a few more minutes – keep stirring to make sure that you coat the rice in the green paste.

8 Add the stock, bring to a simmer (see Glossary, page 122) and then cover the pan with the lid. Cook gently for 14 minutes.

9 **Ask an adult to help you** take the pan off the hob, then leave the rice (with the lid still on) for another 10 minutes to finish cooking. Serve with fish or chicken.

pesto

If you have a pestle and mortar it is great fun bashing the herbs and cheese together. Alternatively, whiz everything in a food processor but **ask an adult to help you.**

1 Peel the garlic and put it in a mortar or food processor with a small pinch of salt (this will help you to squash the garlic). Take the pestle and squash the garlic against the mortar.

2 Add the basil and bash the leaves (or whiz if you are using the food processor).

3 Add the pine nuts and bash (or whiz) again. If you are using a pestle and mortar you will need to take it in turns with friends or family to help you bash everything to stop your arm from aching! It will take a good few minutes.

4 Add the Parmesan and mix together just with a spoon.

5 Spoon the mixture into a bowl and gradually add the olive oil until the sauce just drops off your spoon. Hey presto! You've made pesto!

ingredients

½ clove of garlic

a small pinch of salt

4 handfuls of fresh basil leaves

a big handful of pine nuts

2 handfuls of grated Parmesan cheese

about 2–3 tablespoons olive oil

**makes enough for
2 saucepans of pasta**

COOK IT

herby marinade

This quick marinade will add lots of flavour to chicken or fish. Don't leave it to marinate for longer than 30 minutes as the lemon juice will start to 'cook' the meat or fish.

ingredients

4 chicken pieces (or fish fillets)

for the marinade

a big bunch of fresh herbs e.g. rosemary, parsley, mint, thyme or a combination of these

juice of 1 lemon or lime

3 tablespoons olive oil

1 clove of garlic, peeled and crushed with a garlic crusher

makes enough for 4

1 Using scissors, snip the leaves of the herbs into small pieces and put into a big bowl. Add the lemon or lime juice, olive oil and garlic and stir. Add the chicken or fish, cover the bowl with clingfilm, put in the fridge and leave to marinate for up to 30 minutes. Do not leave it for longer as the marinade can start to change the texture of the chicken or fish and it may fall apart when it is cooked.

2 Turn the oven on to 180˚C (350˚F) Gas 4. Take the chicken or fish out of the marinade, put into a heavy-based roasting dish and cook in the oven for 10 minutes for fish or 15–20 minutes for chicken, or until cooked through – the cooking time will depend on the size of the chicken/fish pieces. **Ask an adult to help you** check that it is cooked all the way through.

3 This is lovely served with some salad leaves and some cherry tomatoes that you have grown in the garden.

Always remember to wash your hands well after touching raw meat or fish.

creamy spinach pasta

Ask an adult to help you cook the pasta and this sauce. It is quick and easy and tastes delicious. This recipe idea came from a child at a local school.

1

5

7

1 Fill a big saucepan with water, put on the hob and **ask an adult to help you** turn on the heat. Bring to the boil (see Glossary, page 122), then **ask an adult to help you** add the pasta and look at the pack instructions for how long to cook it. When it is cooked, **ask an adult to help** you drain the pasta.

2 Using scissors, cut the spinach (or chard) into small pieces or tear with your hands.

3 **Ask an adult to help you** heat the butter and olive oil in your big saucepan. Add the chopped spinach (or chard), put the lid on and cook for a minute.

4 Take the lid off and stir, then put the lid back on for another minute until the spinach has wilted. Lower the heat.

5 Pour the cream onto the spinach, add the Parmesan and stir together.

6 Add a little nutmeg and possibly some freshly ground black pepper and taste to check you like the flavour.

7 **Ask an adult to help you** pour the drained spinach back into the pan over the spinach. Mix everything together. You might like to sprinkle more cheese over the top before you serve it.

ingredients

about 400 g pasta of your choice or as much as you think your family will eat (we like using linguine because it is long and thin and is great fun to eat!)

400 g baby spinach (or chard) leaves

2 teaspoons butter

2 teaspoons olive oil

200 ml double cream

75 g grated Parmesan cheese

a good pinch of freshly grated nutmeg or freshly ground black pepper

makes enough for 4

COOK IT

potatoes, carrots & onions

planting potatoes

Choose your potatoes

Potato plants need a lot of space to grow so before you start planting, take some time to decide where you can grow them.

There are so many types of potato to choose from! Potatoes are also called 'tubers' (see Glossary, page 122).

I think it is a good idea to start by planting the early varieties of potato that will be ready to cook and eat in the summer. Look out for potatoes that are called 'earlies'. This way you can enjoy eating some freshly dug and cooked potatoes with some freshly picked and cooked peas in the same meal. If you have grown some mint you could also pick a few leaves, chop into small pieces and sprinkle over the top of both the peas and potoates.

There are lots of different varieties of early potatoes. You could always try growing a couple of different types of potatoes this year and then grow something different next year.

One thing to know about potatoes is that they are either waxy (which means that they have a firm, slightly waxy texture) or floury (which means that their texture is slightly softer and as its name suggests, more floury).

Chitting

First you need to sprout your potatoes – this is called 'chitting'. You can start this as early as late winter. Put the potatoes in empty egg cartons with the 'eyes' facing upwards (see picture opposite, top left). These eyes will start to sprout. Keep them

in a cool, light room, for example by a back door or near a windowsill. After about 6 weeks you should have some strong green shoots a couple of centimetres long. They are now ready for planting. You can plant them in the garden soil or in big pots outside.

Planting in the garden

1 PREPARE THE SOIL

Rake the top of the soil to break up any lumps. Spread a layer of well-rotted manure or your own compost over the soil and have fun digging it into the soil.

2 DIG A HOLE

You can start planting in early spring and you can plant straight into the ground. Dig a hole in the soil about 10 cm deep with your trowel.

3 PLANT THE POTATOES

Plant one potato with its green shoots facing upwards. If you have the space, make another hole about 20–30 cm away (and ideally leave about 60 cm between rows) and plant another potato.

4 EARTHING UP

Use your trowel to cover the potatoes with the soil. You will need to keep 'earthing up' the potatoes as they grow (see page 38). You can also throw leaves, grass cuttings and soil on top – anything to help cover the shoots.

Planting in pots

You can also plant potatoes in big pots or dustbins. They will need to be deep enough

for you to keep 'earthing up' the potatoes as they grow (see page 38).

1 PICK A POT

Choose a pot with holes in the bottom – the water needs to be able to drain out of the pot. Put some broken pots, shells or small stones in the bottom of the pots – this helps to stop the potatoes from getting waterlogged (too watery).

2 ADD SOIL

Half-fill the pot with a general-purpose potting compost and use your trowel to dig a little hole in the centre of the compost for the potato.

3 PLANT THE POTATOES

Plant a few potatoes with their green shoots facing upwards with a space about the size of an adult's hand between them, then cover with compost.

4 EARTHING UP

Use your trowel to cover the potatoes with the soil. You will need to keep 'earthing up' the potatoes as they grow (see page 38). You can also throw leaves, grass cuttings and soil on top – anything to help cover the shoots.

Not all types of potato will flower, but if the ones you have chosen do start to produce flowers (see picture opposite, bottom right), then it means that your potatoes are ready to harvest.

planting spring onions

It's easiest to grow red and golden onions from 'sets', which are mini onions (see Glossary, page 122), while spring onions can be grown from seed, and in smaller spaces.

You can sow spring onion seeds from beginning to mid-spring.

1 CHOOSE A SPACE
Choose a sunny, sheltered spot.

2 PREPARE THE SOIL
Rake the top of the soil to break up any lumps. Spread a layer of well-rotted manure or your own compost over the soil and have fun digging it into the soil.

3 DIG A HOLE
Drag a trowel along the soil to make a small furrow 1 cm deep.

4 SOW THE SEEDS
Tip some seeds into your hand, then sow the seeds in a single line along the furrow.

5 WATER THE SEEDS
Water the seeds with a special watering can that just sprinkles water gently – if you pour too much water onto the soil in a gush it might wash the seeds away!

6 SOW MORE SEEDS
Ideally you need to leave about 10 cm in between each row of spring onions to give them space to grow.

7 THIN THE SEEDLINGS
When you see green shoots a few centimetres long growing out of the soil, you'll need to 'thin' (see Glossary, page 122) the seedlings so that they are 3 cm apart in the furrow. This will ensure that they have the room to grow bigger.

8 REPLANT THE SEEDLINGS
Take the seedlings you've removed and replant them in the garden soil or in a pot so that they can grow nice and fat. Or you can use them straightaway in a salad or sandwich, even if they seem very thin and little.

planting onions & carrots

Red and golden onions

1 CHOOSE A SPACE
Choose a sunny, sheltered spot.

2 PREPARE THE SOIL
Rake the top of the soil to break up any lumps. Spread a layer of well-rotted manure or your own compost over the soil and have fun digging it into the soil.

3 DIG A HOLE
Drag a trowel along the soil to make a small furrow about the same depth as the size of the onion 'sets'.

4 PLANT THE SETS
Plant the 'sets' with their roots facing down, about 8–10 cm apart. Pat the soil around the onions so that the tips are just visible.

5 PLANT MORE SETS
Ideally you need to leave about 20 cm in between each row of onions to give them space to grow.

Carrots

1 CHOOSE A SPACE
Carrots need to be in a sunny position with a light, well-drained soil. If your soil seems too 'claggy' (which means 'not light enough', see Glossary, page 122), then it might be better to grow the carrots in pots.

2 PREPARE THE SOIL
For carrots you need what gardeners call a fine 'tilth' (see Glossary, page 122). This just means that you need to rake the soil to make sure that it doesn't have any big lumps. Just like with other vegetables you will need to spread a layer of well-rotted manure or your own compost over the soil and have fun digging it into the soil. You should then rake the soil again to make sure that it is fine, without big lumps.

3 DIG A HOLE
Drag a trowel along the soil to make a small furrow 1 cm deep.

4 SOW THE SEEDS
Tip some seeds into your hand, then sow the seeds as thinly as possible – at least 1 cm apart if you can. This is tricky and you will have to be patient and not rush. If you do sow too many seeds, later you will have to 'thin out' (see Glossary, page 122) the carrots that are too close together, but my grandad always said that if you thin the carrots too often the smell from the carrots can attract carrot fly.

5 WATER THE SEEDS
Water the seeds with a special watering can that just sprinkles water gently – if you pour too much water onto the soil in a big gush it might wash the seeds away!

6 SOW MORE SEEDS
Ideally you need to leave about 15 cm in between each row of carrots to give them space to grow. If you have the space in your garden save some seeds for later and sow a few more rows in 2 or 3 weeks' time. This way your carrots should last for a while, instead of all coming at once and then finishing. You can sow carrots until the beginning of the summer.

growing potatoes, carrots & onions

Always remember to label your rows or pots to remind you what is growing and where you planted it!

Potatoes

You can't watch potatoes growing as they are under the ground, which makes it all the more exciting when you dig them up. It's almost like a lucky dip as you are not sure quite what you will find!

When the shoots (green leaves) have grown above the soil to about 15 cm high you will need to 'earth up' your potatoes. This simply means to pile soil around the plant so that you can only see a few centimetres of the green shoots above the ground. Use a trowel or small spade to help dig the soil from the middle of your potato rows to pile it around the tubers (potatoes).

This is really important. You need to keep piling earth around the plants to keep the tubers under the ground in the dark. If light gets to them they can turn green and then become poisonous.

Keep an eye on your potatoes just in case the earth is washed away in the rain. To help prevent this from happening, try not to make the earth piles around the leaves too steep!

You will probably need to 'earth up' 3 or 4 times during the growing season.

Carrots

Carrots need to be 'thinned' while they are growing. This simply means pulling out some of the carrots to give space to the other carrots so that they can grow properly. So when your carrot leaves are about 2.5 cm tall you can pull out some of the small carrots so that the ones left have room around them to grow.

You can eat these small seedlings – they won't need to be cooked. Just add them raw to salads or take them to school in your packed lunchbox. If you think they are too small to eat, add them to your compost heap.

Since you now know that carrots don't like being crowded, it is best to remove any weeds from the soil around them.

It is quite hard pulling out weeds from around carrots – you need to be very gentle and make sure that you don't pull out baby carrots at the same time!

Try to keep the carrots' soil nice and moist – they like water, they don't like to be left to dry out.

Remember companion planting (see page 9). You might want to plants some onions near to your carrots. As both the carrot and onion plants grow, they give off very strong scents and these scents may help drive away each other's pests.

Onions and spring onions

Onions need very little attention and they should quite happily grow without you doing very much!

Remember that for spring onions, you may need to thin them to give each one room to grow – see page 36.

harvesting & preparing
potatoes, carrots & onions

If you want to store onions, harvest them and when the skins are rustling dry you can plait them into strings to hang up. If you are storing potatoes, they need to be in perfect condition and thoroughly dried before storing in paper sacks in the dark. If they are not in complete darkness, they turn green and become poisonous.

Potatoes

You should be able to dig up some potatoes about 3 months after planting. You should know that you can 'rob' the plant to get a few potatoes before pulling up the whole plant. Simply put your hand into the soil around the plant and rummage around to feel for potatoes.

When flowers appear you can harvest the whole plant but **you might need some help from an adult**. Insert a garden fork deep into the soil towards the plant and ease up the whole plant (see picture, top right). Most of the potatoes should come up with the roots but some might get left behind, so dig around a bit.

The plant must be harvested when the stalks die back. If the plant looks diseased, which can sometimes happen in a wet year, harvest the potatoes immediately to prevent the disease from affecting the tubers under the ground.

New potatoes only need a wash and a gentle scrub and they are ready to cook but if you want to peel them, this is how:

• The first time you use a vegetable peeler it can feel a bit awkward but keep practising and you will soon get the hang of it.

• Hold the potato in one hand and run the peeler over it using your thumb as support. Be careful – the peeler is sharp!

• Turn the potato around and keep peeling until you have finished.

• Put the peelings on the compost heap.

Carrots

About 3 months after sowing carrot seeds, when the carrot greens look strong (see picture on page 38, centre), pull one out of the soil and see how big it is. They can be eaten when you think they are big enough.

You don't need to do much with small carrots before you eat them, just give them a wash and then top and tail them – this means cutting the green, leafy ends and cutting the root end off too.

Most young carrots will just need washing but if there is any scarring or ingrained soil you might need to peel them. This is how to peel them if you need to:

• The first time you use a vegetable peeler it can feel a bit awkward but keep practising and you will soon get the hang of it.

• Hold the carrot at one end and rest the other end on a chopping board.

• Starting halfway down, run the vegetable peeler down the carrot away from your body. **Be careful** – the peeler is sharp!

• Twist the carrot as you peel so that you can peel it all the way around.

• Turn the carrot up the other way and hold the other end while you peel the half that still has its skin on.

• Put the peelings on the compost heap or give them to a pet rabbit!

Onions

When the green leaves begin to brown and fall over pull the onions out of the ground. Pull out alternate onions, to allow the others more space to grow. Lay the onions out in the sun for a few days to allow the skins to dry out, then you can store them.

Spring onions

When they look like they have strong green leaves and white bulbs they are ready to harvest.

5 ways with potatoes

Have you ever eaten freshly dug, cooked new potatoes with some fresh mint? This has to be one of the best things about the summer. They are so delicious and they can be eaten with pretty much anything from a bit of cooked chicken or fish to an omelette. When the potatoes are first ready to harvest, I always boil or steam them, but when the season is coming to an end I tend to roast them with some fresh rosemary from the garden. Why don't you try the different ways and see which you prefer.

1 BOILED NEW POTATOES WITH MINT

Using the 'bridge' cutting technique (see page 11), cut any big potatoes in half so that they are all roughly the same size. Put the potatoes and a sprig or two of fresh mint into a small saucepan. Pour water over the top – just enough to cover them. **Ask an adult to help you** turn on the hob. Bring to the boil, then keep boiling the potatoes for 10 minutes. **Ask an adult to help you** test the potatoes with a skewer. When they are ready, the skewer should easily glide into them. Serve with a little butter.

2 STEAMED NEW POTATOES

Using the 'bridge' cutting technique (see page 11), cut any big potatoes in half so that they are all roughly the same size. Half-fill a saucepan with water. Put the potatoes into a colander or steamer inside the pan (the bottom of the colander/steamer should be above the water). Put the lid on the pan. **Ask an adult to help you** turn on the hob. Bring the water to the boil, then steam the potatoes for 10 minutes. **Ask an adult to help you** test the potatoes with a skewer. When they are ready, the skewer should easily glide into them.

3 ROASTED NEW POTATOES

Turn the oven on to 190°C (375°F) Gas 5. Using the 'bridge' cutting technique (see page 11), cut any big potatoes in half so that they are all roughly the same size. Put them into a big, heavy-based roasting tin. Drizzle a little olive oil over the top. Add 2 cloves of garlic (with their skin on) and sprigs of rosemary. Using your oven gloves put the tin into the oven and roast for 20 minutes. **Ask an adult to help you** take the tin out of the oven and move the potatoes around with a wooden spoon. Roast a little longer if they are still not ready.

4 NEW POTATO & CHIVE SALAD

You will need some boiled or steamed new potatoes ready before you start this salad. Make sure they are all roughly the same size – cut any big potatoes in half using the 'bridge' cutting technique (see page 11). Put the potatoes into a bowl. In a separate, small bowl mix together equal amounts of natural yoghurt and mayonnaise – about 2 tablespoons of each for a big bowl of potatoes. Using scissors, snip some chives into small pieces and add to the potato salad with the yoghurt mix.

5 MASHED NEW POTATOES

You can either make mash from scratch by peeling some new potatoes, then boiling or steaming them as described earlier. Or you can use already cooked new potatoes, in which case you will need to rub the cooled potatoes all over with your hands to remove the skin. Put the potatoes into a bowl. Hold a potato masher in your hand, add a small amount of butter and start squashing and mashing. If you have used cold potatoes then you will need to heat the mash in the microwave.

5 ways with carrots

Freshly pulled small carrots don't need anything other than a quick wash. They are sweet and delicious on their own or with a simple dip. I know children who prefer carrots raw all the time, not just as a snack, but also as part of a meal. Even if this is the case it is a life skill to learn how to cook vegetables properly. There will be a time when you need to cook carrots and it is a good idea to learn how to do this well. Cooked vegetables should still have some 'bite', which means that they should not be too soft. This is not just important for the flavour of the vegetable, it is also vital to help keep some of their good 'nutrients' (the things that help keep us healthy), inside the carrots – we don't want to cook these all away.

1 GRATED CARROT SALAD

Put a cheese grater on a chopping board and hold firmly by its handle. With your other hand hold a peeled carrot at its widest end and, keeping your fingers well away from the grater, grate the carrot by rubbing it up and down the grater. Keep grating until you are left with a small end of carrot but watch your finger and knuckles don't get caught on the 'teeth' of the grater. Mix some grated carrots with grated apple, raisins, a little natural yoghurt and mayonnaise for an easy, refreshing salad.

2 STEAMED CARROTS

Wash the carrots if they are small, or peel them if their skin is very thick or ingrained with dirt (see page 41). Using the 'claw' cutting technique (see page 11), slice the carrots into thin circles. Half-fill a saucepan with water. Put the carrots into a colander or steamer inside the pan (the bottom of the colander/steamer should be above the water). Put the lid on the pan. **Ask an adult to help you** turn on the hob. Bring the water to the boil, then steam the carrots for about 3–4 minutes.

5 WAYS

3 BOILED CARROTS

Wash the carrots if they are small, or peel them if their skin is very thick or ingrained with dirt (see page 41). Using the 'claw' cutting technique (see page 11), slice the carrots into thin circles, then put into a small saucepan. Pour water over the top – just enough to cover them. **Ask an adult to help you** turn on the hob. Bring to the boil, then keep boiling the carrots for 3–4 minutes. **Ask an adult to help you** test the carrots with a skewer. When they are ready, the skewer should easily glide into them but they should still be firm.

4 RAW CARROTS & DIP

Peel the carrots using a vegetable peeler (see page 41). Using the 'claw' cutting technique (see page 11), cut the carrots in half across the middle. Using the 'bridge' cutting technique (see page 11), cut the carrot halves into thin strips. Mix together an equal amount of cream cheese and natural yoghurt. Using scissors carefully snip a bunch of fresh herbs (like chives, parsley and mint) into small pieces. Add the herbs to the cream cheese and mix everything together.

5 ROASTED YOUNG CARROTS

Turn the oven on to 200°C (400°F) Gas 7. Using the 'claw' cutting technique (see page 11), cut the carrots in half or thirds. Using the 'bridge' cutting technique (see page 11), cut the carrot pieces in half lengthways. Put them into a roasting tin and drizzle with olive oil. Using your oven gloves put the tin into the oven and roast for 15 minutes. **Ask an adult to help you** take the tin out of the oven. Drizzle 2 tablespoons of honey over the top and add a sprig of rosemary. Using oven gloves put back into the oven for 10 minutes.

5 ways with onions

Learning to chop an onion properly is a life skill. So many recipes start with a chopped onion. Once you have learnt how to do this there are so many things that you can cook. It doesn't matter if the onion pieces are not small and perfectly sized – the important thing is to have a go. You may find it easier to cut an onion into slices. This is fine if it means that you can make the recipe yourself. Always remember to be **near an adult** when you are using a knife.

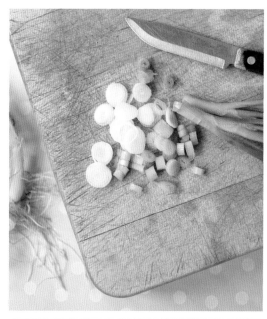

1 HOW TO SLICE SPRING ONIONS

Using the 'claw' cutting technique (see page 11), trim the ends off the spring onions. Using the 'claw' cutting technique again, slice the onions into thin circles. When you first start cutting, don't worry if the slices are different thicknesses, keep practising and you will get better. The white parts of the onions are more strongly flavoured than the green, and a recipe might say that you only need one part. Use the other part in salad, if you like.

2 HOW TO CUT ONION WEDGES

Sit the onion on a chopping board and carefully holding it in a 'claw' cutting position (see page 11). Cut off the pointed end. Sit the onion on the board with the flat end (the end that you have just cut) sitting on the board. Hold the onion in a 'bridge' cutting position (see page 11). Cut the onion in half. Peel away the dry, papery skin and thin membrane. Sit one half, flat side down, on the chopping board. Using the 'bridge' cutting technique, cut through the onion 3 or 4 times to make wedges.

3 SOFTENED ONIONS

Slice or dice the onion, following the instructions on this page. **Ask an adult to help you** put a tablespoon of olive or vegetable oil in a saucepan and turn on the hob. Add the onion and cook over gentle heat for at least 5 minutes. Sometimes it takes a bit longer than this to soften the onions. Don't turn the heat up or the onions will go brown – just let them cook gently until they are pale gold and lovely and soft.

4 HOW TO SLICE ONIONS

Hold the onion in a 'bridge' cutting position (see page 11). Cut the onion in half. Peel away the dry, papery skin and thin membrane. Sit one half, flat side down, on the chopping board. Using the 'claw' cutting technique (see page 11), cut across the onion to make slices.

5 HOW TO DICE ONIONS

Hold the onion in a 'bridge' cutting position (see page 11). Cut the onion in half. Peel away the dry, papery skin and thin membrane.

Then, to chop the onion into small pieces – known as 'dice' – use the 'bridge' cutting technique (see page 11). Make lots of cuts in the onion from just above the root end to the top of the onion. Then switch to the 'claw' cutting technique (see page 11) and cut across the onion the other way to make small 'dice'.

potato cakes

This is a great way to use up leftover cooked potatoes. You can eat these with anything but they taste particularly good with bacon and tomatoes. Cook the bacon and tomatoes in the oven at the same time.

ingredients

about 500 g cold cooked potatoes (but you can make them with any amount of leftover potatoes)

a little plain flour

freshly ground black pepper

sunflower oil, for frying

bacon and tomatoes, to serve (optional)

makes enough for 4

1 Turn the oven on to 200°C (400°F) Gas 6. The potatoes need to be peeled – if they still have their skins on, rub them with your hands to get the skins off.

2 Put the potatoes into a bowl. Hold a potato masher in your hand and start squashing and mashing. If you find that the bowl is moving around, put a tea towel underneath it to keep it in place.

3 Add 2 teaspoons of plain flour and a little freshly ground black pepper, if you like it.

4 Break the potato into small balls and then mould each one into rounds. Lightly dip in flour.

5 Brush a heavy-based roasting tin with olive oil and put the potato cakes in the tin. Using oven gloves, put the tin in the oven and roast for 10 minutes. Using oven gloves, take the tin out of the oven and carefully turn the potato cakes over with a spatula. Using oven gloves, put back in the oven for another 10 minutes.

6 You can try these with bacon and tomatoes, cooked in the oven.

COOK IT

roasted onions & sausages

The chipolata sausages in this yummy dinner should go golden brown and the apples and onions will be soft and sweet. Eat with jacket potatoes.

ingredients

3 red or white onions or a mixture of the two

olive oil, for drizzling

4 eating apples

12 good-quality chipolatas or other sausages

4 jacket potatoes (put the potatoes into the oven at the same time so that you have lovely fluffy potatoes to eat with your sausages)

makes enough for 4

1 Turn the oven on to 200°C (400°F) Gas 6.

2 Cut the onions into wedges (see page 46). Scatter the wedges over a heavy-based roasting tin. Drizzle over a little olive oil.

3 Ask an adult to help you core the apples using an apple corer. Using the 'bridge' cutting technique cut the apples in half and then into quarters. Scatter the onion and apple over the roasting tin.

4 Top with sausages. Drizzle with a little more olive oil.

5 Using oven gloves, put the tin in the oven and roast for 20 minutes. Using oven gloves, take the tin out of the oven and turn the sausages over with tongs so that they go brown on both sides. Using oven gloves, put back in the oven for another 15 minutes.

6 Serve with jacket potatoes.

Always remember to wash your hands well after touching raw meat or fish.

potato & onion tortilla

This is almost a complete meal in a pan – all you need is some salad or green vegetables to go with it. You may have many of these ingredients already growing in your garden!

COOK IT

1 Put the potatoes into a small saucepan and pour water over the top – just enough to cover them. **Ask an adult to help you** turn on the hob. Bring to the boil, then lower the heat, cover the pan with the lid and boil for 10 minutes, or until just tender. Drain and leave to cool until the potatoes are cool enough to handle.

2 In the meantime, crack the eggs into a bowl (see page 11). Season with a little freshly ground black pepper, if you like it. Beat lightly with a fork and set aside.

3 **Ask an adult to help you** heat the olive oil in a large frying pan over gentle heat, add the

spring onions and cook very slowly until soft. This will take about 4–5 minutes. Stir the spring onions occasionally with a wooden spoon.

4 Now that the potatoes are colder, rub them with your hands to get the skins off. Cut each potato in half using the 'bridge' cutting technique (see page 11). Cut each half into thick slices using the 'claw' cutting technique (see page 11).

5 Turn the grill on to high.

6 Add the potatoes to the frying pan and cook for a few more minutes. Stir very carefully so that you do not break up the potatoes.

7 Pour the beaten eggs into the pan and stir gently so that the egg covers the bottom of the pan. Turn the heat down to its lowest setting and cook the tortilla (without a lid on) for about 3 minutes until there is only a little runny egg left on the top.

8 Sprinkle the grated cheese all over the top and using oven gloves put the tortilla under the grill for 2 minutes, until the egg is cooked.

9 Leave to cool slightly, then **ask an adult to help you** slide the tortilla out of the pan and onto a chopping board. Cut into squares and serve with salad or steamed green vegetables.

ingredients

3 small potatoes, peeled

5 eggs

2 tablespoons olive oil

2 spring onions, trimmed and sliced
(see page 46)

40 g Cheddar cheese, grated

salad or steamed green vegetables,
to serve

freshly ground black pepper

*a frying pan with a heatproof handle
that you can put under the grill*

makes enough for 4

carrot soup

This tastes really sweet and creamy but it's so easy because you hardly need any ingredients to make it delicious. If you don't like the taste of coconut milk you could use the same amount of vegetable stock instead.

1 Turn the oven on to 180°C (350°F) Gas 4.

2 Peel the carrots and top and tail them (see page 41). Using the 'bridge' cutting technique (see page 11), cut the carrots into big chunks.

3 Cut the onion into wedges (see page 46).

4 Put the onion and carrots into a heavy-based roasting tin, add the garlic and drizzle with a little oil. Using oven gloves, put the tin in the oven and roast for 30 minutes.

5 Ask an adult to help you take the tin out of the oven and using a palette knife carefully turn the vegetables over so that they cook evenly all over.

6 Using oven gloves, take the tin out of the oven and carefully spoon the vegetables into a food processor. Squeeze the roasted garlic clove out of its skin and into the processor. Always **ask an adult to help you** with a food processor and remember that the blade in the middle is as sharp as a knife – never touch it!

7 Add half the coconut milk, put the lid on and **ask an adult** to blend the soup until smooth.

8 Ask an adult to help you pour the puréed soup into a saucepan. Add the rest of the coconut milk and the stock. Add the herbs and heat gently over medium heat. Taste the soup – you might like to add more stock if you want the soup to be thinner in texture.

ingredients

1 kg carrots

1 onion

1 clove of garlic, skin left on

olive oil, for drizzling

a 400-ml tin of coconut milk

400 ml vegetable stock

fresh herbs, e.g. parsley, coriander, snipped with scissors

makes enough for 4

carrot muffins

You need to whisk the eggs and sugar together until they are quite thick and creamy for these little cakes. If you are using a hand whisk this will take time so you might like to pass the whisk to a friend to help you.

3

5

6

1 Turn the oven on to 180°C (350°F) Gas 4. Put 12 paper cases into a muffin tray, or use 12 silicone cases on a baking tray.

2 Peel and grate the carrots (see page 44) using the smaller holes on the grater – you want the carrots to be grated finely so that they mix into the cake mixture easily.

3 Crack the eggs into a large bowl (see page 11). Beat lightly with a fork and set aside.

4 Add the sugar and whisk together with a hand whisk or **ask an adult to help you** use an electric whisk. Whisk until thick and creamy.

5 Gradually add the oil, whisking all the time.

6 Add flour, mixed spice (or cinnamon and nutmeg), coconut and dried fruit and stir until everything's mixed in.

7 Spoon the mixture into the muffin cases and bake in the preheated oven for 12–14 minutes, or until the muffins are cooked and golden.

8 **Ask an adult to help you** take the muffin tray out of the oven and leave to cool a little. Then put the muffins on a cooling rack to cool down until you are ready to eat them.

ingredients

225 g carrots

3 eggs

140 g light brown soft sugar

7 tablespoons sunflower oil

150 g plain or wholemeal self-raising flour (or half and half)

1 teaspoon mixed spice or a mixture of ground cinnamon and nutmeg

70 g desiccated coconut (if you don't like coconut add more dried fruit instead)

75 g mixed dried fruit e.g. raisins, cranberries, blueberries

a muffin tray and 12 paper cases, or 12 silicone muffin cases

makes about 12 muffins

COOK IT

courgettes & tomatoes

planting courgettes & cucumbers

Sow from seed

You can sow courgette and cucumber seeds in a pot in your house at the beginning of spring or in the middle. Hopefully by the end of spring you will then be able to plant them outside in the garden.

1 PICK A POT

Find some small pots: plastic cups or cleaned-out yoghurt pots are ideal. You will need one pot per seed. **Ask an adult** to poke a few holes in the bottom using a skewer or scissors.

2 ADD SOIL

Three-quarters fill the pot with a general-purpose potting compost.

3 SOW THE SEEDS

Put some seeds into one of your hands – you'll see that the seeds for courgettes and cucumbers are flat, not round like others you might have seen. Poke one seed in each pot so that the seed is on its side, not flat down. Press gently into the compost and sprinkle a little more compost over the top. They should germinate (see Glossary, page 122) in about a week.

4 WATER AND WAIT

In about a month you should have a small plant that is ready to be planted straight in the garden or in a big pot outside. It will need to be about 15 cm tall and you should be able to see its roots in the bottom of the pot.

Planting in the garden

If you have the space in your garden to grow your courgettes or cucumbers in the soil, follow these steps.

Ideally about 2 hours before you start the gardening, water your plant in its pot.

5 CHOOSE A SPACE

Wait until the weather is warm, ideally about the end of spring. Choose a sunny, sheltered spot in the garden.

6 PREPARE THE SOIL

Spread a layer of well-rotted manure or your own compost over the soil and have fun digging it into the soil.

7 DIG A HOLE

Dig a hole with your trowel in the soil.

8 TIP THE PLANT OUT

Carefully tip the plant out of the pot and try to keep as much compost around the roots as possible. Put the plant into the hole with its roots facing down.

9 TUCK THE PLANT IN

Fill in more soil around the plant, gently press it down with your hands, then give it a good drink of water.

Cucumbers can sprout and grow across the ground or you can encourage the plant to grow up a cane.

Planting in pots

You can plant the seedlings in a big pot instead of in your garden soil. Follow steps **1**-**4** above, then switch to these steps.

First, about 2 hours before you start the gardening, water your plant in its pot.

5 PICK A POT

Look for a big pot about the size of a bucket (about 30 cm wide at the top).

6 CHOOSE A SPACE

Choose a sunny, sheltered spot for the pot (against a south-facing wall is ideal – ask your parents where they think is best).

7 ADD SOIL

Three-quarters fill the pot with a general-purpose potting compost and use your trowel to dig a little hole in the centre of the compost for the plant.

8 TIP THE PLANT OUT

Carefully tip the plant out of the pot and try to keep as much compost around the roots as possible. Put the plant into the hole with its roots facing down.

9 TUCK THE PLANT IN

Fill in more soil around the plant, gently press it down with your hands, then give it a good drink of water.

planting tomatoes

Sow from seed

Put the seeds in your hand. If you pour seeds straight from the packet into the soil you will get too many seedlings.

1 PICK A POT

Find some small pots: plastic cups or cleaned-out yoghurt pots are ideal. **Ask an adult** to poke a few holes in the bottom using a skewer or scissors.

2 ADD SOIL

Three-quarters fill the pot with a general-purpose potting compost.

3 SOW THE SEEDS

Drop 2 seeds into each pot. Press gently into the compost and put more compost over the top. They should germinate (see Glossary, page 122) in about a week.

4 PULL OUT A SEEDLING

When the seedlings are about 2 cm high, pull out the weakest one (if they have both germinated), leaving just one in each pot.

In about 3 weeks you should have a small plant that is ready to be planted straight in the garden or in a big pot outside. You should be able to see its roots in the bottom of the pot.

Planting in the garden

If you have the space in your garden to grow your tomatoes in the soil, follow these steps.

Ideally about 2 hours before you start the gardening, water your plant in its pot.

5 CHOOSE A SPACE

Choose a sunny, sheltered spot.

6 PREPARE THE SOIL

Spread a layer of well-rotted manure or your own compost over the soil and have fun digging it into the soil.

7 DIG A HOLE

Dig a hole with your trowel in the soil.

8 TIP THE PLANT OUT

Carefully tip the plant out of the pot and try to keep as much compost around the roots as possible. Put the plant into the hole with its roots facing down.

9 TUCK THE PLANT IN

Fill in more soil around the plant, gently press it down with your hands, then give it a good drink of water.

Planting in pots

You can plant the seedlings in a big pot instead of in the garden soil. Follow steps **1-4** above, then switch to these steps.

5 PICK A POT

Look for a big pot about the size of a bucket (about 30 cm wide at the top).

6 CHOOSE A SPACE

Choose a sunny, sheltered spot for the pot (against a south-facing wall is ideal – ask your parents where they think is best).

7 ADD SOIL

Three-quarters fill the pot with a general-purpose potting compost and use your

trowel to dig a little hole in the centre of the compost for the plant.

8 TIP THE PLANT OUT

Carefully tip the plant out of the pot and try to keep as much compost around the roots as possible. Put the plant into the hole with its roots facing down.

9 TUCK THE PLANT IN

Fill in more soil around the plant, gently press it down with your hands, then give it a good drink of water.

growing courgettes & tomatoes

Courgettes & cucumbers

Make sure you water your courgettes and cucumbers regularly. Try to water the soil around the plant, not over it, as too much water on the plant can cause it to rot.

If you have some straw, gently rest some around the plants: this helps to stop weeds from growing and to keep the water in the soil so the plants stay moist and happy.

When the courgette plant flowers on the tip of the growing courgette, you can pick the flowers, cook them and eat them. Just fry them in a little olive oil, then add them to pasta or risotto. If you leave the flower it will gradually shrivel and drop off.

There are so many types of courgette plant that will produce courgettes of all shapes and sizes – have fun watching yours grow.

Tomatoes

Make sure that you only put your tomato seedlings outside in the garden once all the frost has finished and the weather is warmer – they don't like getting cold.

Water tomato plants once a day – this is especially important if you are growing them in pots. When you water tomato plants, aim the watering can at the bottom of the plant. Try not to water the leaves as this can spread disease.

To help make sure that the tomatoes have enough water you could try 'hilling'. This means simply making a small hill of soil around the tomato stems. This helps to keep the water in the soil for the plants to drink. Use your trowel to pile the soil around the stems.

Pinch off the side shoots that grow where the leaf stalks join the stem – this makes the plant grow stronger.

Ask your garden centre for advice about the best organic liquid feed for tomatoes growing in pots. Feed them once a week after the plants have flowered.

Watch the flowers grow on the plants. If you are lucky, each flower should form a tomato! Tomatoes will swell and grow fat! Hopefully if you have enough sunshine they will turn red quickly and then they'll be ready to pick.

Each bunch of tomatoes is called a truss.

Some plants need a cane to help support the plant. Push a cane into the middle of the pot and then you will need to **ask an adult to help you** tie a piece of string around the stem and the cane. You won't need to do this for bush tomato plants. As their name suggests, they are smaller bushier plants that don't need any support.

If you like, you can use your own tomato or cucumber seeds to grow your next crop. Scoop the seeds out of a ripe tomato or cucumber and put them on kitchen paper to dry out for a few days. Store them in a paper bag in the cupboard (somewhere dark and dry) until you are ready to sow.

harvesting & preparing courgettes & tomatoes

It's easy to see when tomatoes are ready to harvest: they turn red! For courgettes and cucumbers, you should keep an eye on their size and that will tell you when they are ready. You will **need an adult to help you** pick the ripe courgettes.

Courgettes

Some people pick their courgettes when they are really small, just 4–5 cm long, and lots of children like them when they are this small. I think they have a little more flavour when they are slightly bigger than this – about 6–10 cm long (a bit like a sausage).

This is one vegetable that you will **need an adult to help you** pick. They are too tough to just pull from the plant and if you did just pull them you would probably pull the whole plant out of the ground! You will **need an adult** to cut them away from the plant using a sharp knife. Try not to damage the plant or any of the other courgettes at the same time!

If you see any damaged courgettes, cut them away from the plant and put them on your compost heap. You may need to pick courgettes every day in order to stop them from getting too big.

If you leave them on the plant for too long they will get bigger and bigger. I know a lot of children who don't enjoy eating big courgettes nearly as much as they like eating small courgettes. Courgettes can have less flavour and taste slightly watery if they are left until they are too big.

Wash your courgettes and then top and tail them – this means cutting off both ends of the courgette. You will need to do this with a small sharp knife and use the 'claw' cutting technique (see page 11). You can then slice them and eat them raw or cook the courgettes first – see pages 66 and 67.

Cucumbers

As soon as your cucumbers are about 15 cm long, you can start picking them. Don't leave them on the plant for too long – the bigger the cucumber, the tougher and more bitter it can become.

Wash your cucumber and then top and tail it if you are planning to use the whole thing at once. If you think you will only use a bit of it, only chop one end off. You will need to do this with a small sharp knife and use the 'claw' cutting technique (see page 11).

Cucumbers should keep for at least a week in the salad drawer of the fridge.

Tomatoes

Pick a tomato by pulling the tomato and its stalk off the plant.

Ideally, only pick tomatoes when they are ripe, but did you know that if you pick a tomato before it is ready to eat and leave it in a warm place like your kitchen, it will ripen and turn red?

When you have picked the tomatoes, keep them out of the fridge. They are not happy being cold and they won't taste so good.

If you pick them when they are really red and juicy but you are not ready to eat them, to stop them from going too ripe and then turning bad you will need to keep them in a cool (but not cold) place, like a vegetable rack in a cupboard. Try to find somewhere that is cooler than the kitchen.

You don't need to do much to tomatoes before you eat them. Just give them a quick wash, pull the stalks off and eat the lovely tomatoes. If you want the tomatoes to look pretty on the table, you might like to leave them on their stalks (see picture, bottom right). Do the same if you want to roast the tomatoes.

5 ways with courgettes

Small, sweet home-grown courgettes taste totally different to large shop-bought courgettes, which can be horribly flavourless. My children refused to eat courgettes until we started to grow them. They are even good raw: try peeling or grating them and adding them to salads. Make a lovely lemony dressing and drizzle this over the top, it really does taste good. Hopefully you will have few courgettes from one plant so you should be able to enjoy several ways of eating them.

1 COURGETTE RIBBONS

The best way to do this is with a vegetable peeler. Hold the courgette at one end and rest the other end on a chopping board. Starting halfway down, run the vegetable peeler down the courgette away from your body. **Be careful** – the peeler is sharp! Twist the courgette as you peel. Turn the courgette up the other way and hold the other end while you peel thin ribbons from the other half. Add the ribbons to a salad.

2 STEAMED COURGETTES

Put the courgette onto a chopping board and, using the 'claw' cutting technique (see page 11), slice the courgette into thin circles. Half-fill a saucepan with water. Put the slices into a colander or steamer inside the pan (the bottom of the colander/steamer should be above the water). Put the lid on the pan. **Ask an adult to help you** turn on the hob. Bring the water to the boil, then steam the courgettes for 3–4 minutes or until a small knife easily slides through them.

3 HOW TO SLICE COURGETTES

Put the courgette onto a chopping board and, using the 'claw' cutting technique (see page 11), slice the courgette into thin circles. Keep sliding your fingers back as your slice the courgette.

4 FRIED COURGETTES

Put the courgette onto a chopping board and, using the 'claw' cutting technique (see page 11), slice the courgette into thin circles. Keep sliding your fingers back as your slice the courgette. **Ask an adult to help you** heat a little vegetable oil and a small piece of butter in a frying pan, add the courgettes and fry for a few minutes until just golden. **Ask an adult to help you** test the courgettes with a fork. When they are ready, the fork should easily glide into them but they should still be firm.

5 CUCUMBER TOPPERS

Using the 'bridge' cutting technique (see page 11), cut the cucumber into thirds, then cut each third in half lengthways. Using a teaspoon, scoop the seeds out of the cucumber. Spread some peanut butter in the middle of the cucumber where the seeds used to be and serve!

cooking with courgettes & tomatoes

5 ways with tomatoes

Did you know that a tomato is really a fruit, not a vegetable? Fruits grow from inside the flower of the plant. The fruit also contains the seeds from the plant. Vegetables tend to be other parts of the plant like the leaves, the stalks or the roots. The thing about tomatoes that confuses us is that we normally use them in savoury food, not sweet food like other fruits. If you have tomatoes on your plant that just won't seem to ripen you may want to pick them and have a go at this trick: put the under-ripe tomatoes into a paper bag with a ripe tomato and leave them at room temperature. The under-ripe tomatoes should gradually turn ripe!

1 CHERRY TOMATOES FOR LUNCHBOXES

It is not really surprising that tomatoes are a fruit – they are certainly sweet and great to eat on their own. Next time you have a packed lunch at school, put a few ripe cherry tomatoes in a tub to eat with your sandwich. And here's another idea: have you tried eating a really ripe juicy tomato with a piece of cheese and cucumber? They taste great together and they're so easy to prepare for your lunchbox in the morning before school!

2 STUFFED TOMATOES

Using the 'bridge' cutting technique (see page 11), carefully cut the top off the tomatoes so that you end up with a sort of lid. Scoop out the seeds and the middle of the tomatoes with a teaspoon. Put a little cream cheese into a small bowl. Using scissors, snip some chives or other fresh herbs into small pieces and add to the cream cheese. Stir together, then using the teaspoon again, fill the tomatoes with the herby cream cheese.

5 WAYS

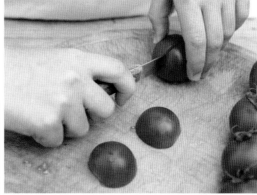

3 THREE–COLOUR SALAD

Using the 'bridge' cutting technique (see page 11), slice the tomatoes into three circles or halve them if you find that easier. Put them in a little salad bowl. If you have some mozzarella cheese, tear it into pieces and scatter over the tomatoes. Top with some fresh basil leaves and drizzle a little olive oil over everything. That's got to be the easiest salad in the world!

4 HOW TO CHOP TOMATOES

You will need a small sharp knife for cutting tomatoes, so be very careful when you are using it. Put the tomato onto a chopping board and, using the 'bridge' cutting technique (see page 11), cut into the tomato by pressing the knife into it. Sometimes it's hard to cut the skin of the tomato, that's why you need a good sharp knife. Then put one half of a tomato, cut side down, on the chopping board. Using the 'bridge' cutting technique cut the tomato half in half again to make quarters.

5 ROASTED TOMATOES

My eldest daughter much prefers eating roasted tomatoes than raw ones. This is her recipe. Turn the oven on to 180°C (350°F) Gas 4. Put lots of ripe cherry tomatoes into a roasting tin. Drizzle over a little olive oil and add 2 cloves of garlic (skin left on) and a sprig of fresh rosemary. Using your oven gloves put the tin into the oven and roast for 35 minutes. When they are ready to come out of the oven they look wrinkled. We like to eat them with a piece of meat and potatoes or rice.

easy tomato tarts

Puff pastry is so easy to use, just roll it, cut out shapes and top with your favourite toppings to make easy tarts. Use sun-dried tomato paste or olive tapenade under your topping.

2   **4**   **5**

1 Turn the oven on to 200°C (400°F) Gas 6.

2 Sprinkle some flour on a clean work surface. Roll out the puff pastry on the work surface and cut into 6 evenly sized squares or rectangles.

3 Grease a baking tray and put the pastry squares onto the tray.

4 Spread a little sun-dried tomato paste or olive tapenade over the pastry but try to leave the very edges bare.

5 Arrange the sliced tomatoes over the tomato paste and try to place them in a layer rather than piling them up.

6 Tear the mozzarella cheese into little pieces and put some on top of the tomatoes.

7 Using oven gloves, put the tray in the oven and roast for 15 minutes or until the pastry is golden and puffed up and the mozzarella has melted.

8 Ask an adult to help you take the tray out of the oven and sprinkle with fresh basil leaves.

ingredients

375 g ready-rolled puff pastry

4 tablespoons sun-dried tomato paste or olive tapenade

20 cherry tomatoes, each one sliced into 3

1 ball of mozzarella cheese or 4 handfuls of grated Parmesan cheese

a handful of fresh basil leaves

makes 4 tarts

COOK IT

pizza toast

You can be as creative as you like with these and use up anything you have in your fridge. Alternatively, keep them simple and use tomatoes, herbs and cheese. These are great for lunch or a snack after school.

1 Turn on the grill.

2 Put the bread slices on a baking tray. Using oven gloves put the tray under the grill and toast until golden on one side. **Ask an adult to help you** take the tray out of the grill. Leave the toast to cool slightly.

3 Turn the toast over, then spread the other side with tomato purée and top with tomatoes.

4 If you want to add some of the other optional toppings, scatter them over the top now.

5 Using scissors, snip the herbs into small pieces and sprinkle over the top.

6 Sprinkle with the grated cheese and **ask an adult to help you** put the tray back under the grill until the cheese has melted.

ingredients

4 thick slices of bread
(or French baguette)

4 tablespoons tomato purée

8 cherry tomatoes,
each one sliced into 3

optional toppings e.g. chopped ham
or tinned tuna, tinned sweetcorn or
chopped peppers

a handful of fresh parsley or other
fresh herb

4 handfuls of grated Cheddar cheese

makes 4 toasts

COOK IT

courgette salad

My children prefer eating courgettes raw instead of cooked. If you're the same, try making this simple salad – and at the same time, practise making courgette ribbons!

ingredients

2 courgettes

4 big handfuls of salad leaves e.g. rocket, baby spinach or chard or a combination of these

2 tablespoons pine nuts (or pumpkin or sunflower seeds)

a handful of fresh herbs, if you like

for the dressing

2 teaspoons lemon juice

2 tablespoons olive oil

makes enough for 4

1 Make the courgette ribbons (see page 66).

2 Wash the salad leaves and put them into a big salad bowl. Scatter the courgette ribbons over the top.

3 In a glass jar or small jug mix together the lemon juice and olive oil for the dressing and drizzle over the salad. Toss everything together with salad serving spoons.

4 Sprinkle the pine nuts or seeds over the top. If you like you can sprinkle some snipped fresh herbs over the top too.

courgette stir-fry

To 'stir-fry' means exactly that – you stir the food in the pan while you fry it. The key to a good stir-fry is to chop all the vegetables first and get all the ingredients ready – once you start 'stir-frying' it is all very quick!

1 To cut the courgettes, follow the instructions on page 45 for cutting carrots into matchsticks (for eating with a dip). You want long, thin sticks – not circles – of courgette to match the shape of the greens beans so that everything cooks at the same speed.

2 Ask an adult to help you heat the sesame and vegetable oils in a heavy-based frying pan or wok, then add the onion and fry for a few minutes until it looks soft and pale gold.

3 Add the ginger, garlic, courgette and green beans to the pan and fry for another few minutes. Keep mixing everything so that it cooks evenly.

4 Add the soy sauce and continue to stir fry, tossing everything together.

5 If you'd like to add some herbs, using scissors, snip the herbs into small pieces and scatter over the top.

6 Add the cooked noodles or rice to the pan and stir through until nicely mixed.

7 The great thing about stir-fries is that you can use almost any vegetable you like, as long as you cut them the same size. Try some home-grown carrots, red onions or spring onions. You can also add beansprouts for extra crunch. Experiment with different seasonings like Chinese five-spice or if you like a bit of heat, add a little fresh or dried chilli.

COOK IT

ingredients

2 courgettes

2 teaspoons sesame oil

2 teaspoons vegetable oil

1 onion, peeled, halved and sliced
(see page 47)

a small piece of root ginger, grated
(see instructions for grated carrots
on page 44)

1 clove of garlic, peeled and crushed
with a garlic crusher

2 large handfuls of green beans

a little reduced-salt soy sauce

a large of handful fresh herbs e.g.
parsley or mint, if you like

freshly cooked, hot egg noodles or
rice, to serve

makes enough for 4

salad & cream cheese sandwiches

Have you ever had a go at spreading something onto bread? It is great fun. Try spreading cream cheese onto bread and then top with lots of crunchy ingredients for a yummy sandwich.

1 To slice the cucumber, follow the instructions on page 67 for slicing courgettes.

2 Using the 'bridge' cutting technique (see page 11), cut the tomatoes into slices.

3 Take the slices of bread and put them on the clean work surface or chopping board. Using a table knife (this is blunt, not sharp like a kitchen knife), spread some cream cheese over a slice of bread, holding the knife almost flat above the bread to help you spread the cheese. Spread some cheese on the other slice of bread too. This will help the sandwich filling to stick and stay in the sandwich!

4 Put the cucumber and tomato slices on one slice of bread, then top with spinach, chard or lettuce.

5 Put the other slice of bread over the top. Cut the sandwich in half or quarters.

ingredients

a small piece of cucumber

a few cherry tomatoes

2 slices of bread of your choice

a little cream cheese

a few spinach leaves, chard or lettuce or a combination of these

makes 1 sandwich

COOK IT

couscous salad

This recipe is based on one by a chef called Peter Vaughan who runs a cookery school. Peter held a workshop in my marquee at the Children's Food Festival.

1 Ask an adult to help you put the sunflower oil in a large saucepan over medium heat, then add the couscous and spices and heat until the couscous has turned a deep golden colour.

2 Remove the pan from the heat. Ask an adult to help you pour the boiling vegetable stock over the couscous, then cover with the pan lid and leave for 10 minutes.

3 After 10 minutes, the couscous should have absorbed all of the stock. Stir it around with a fork to make the couscous grains nice and fluffy.

4 Mix in all the other ingredients and serve!

ingredients

1 tablespoon sunflower oil

200 g couscous

a pinch each of ground cumin, coriander and turmeric

350 ml boiling vegetable stock (or just enough to cover the couscous – see step 1 of the method)

a 400-g tin of chickpeas, drained

a small tin of sweetcorn, drained

2 carrots peeled and grated (see page 44)

a handful of baby spinach

2 spring onions, sliced (see page 46)

2 tomatoes, chopped (see page 59)

juice of ½ a lemon

1 tablespoon olive oil

makes enough for 4

chocolate & courgette cake

It might seem crazy to put courgettes in a cake but they help to keep this cake moist. Make some and then give some slices to friends and see if they can work out what is in it! I bet they don't guess courgette!

COOK IT

1 Turn the oven on to 180°C (350°F) Gas 4. Cut a piece of greaseproof paper the width of your cake tin and a little bit longer. Lay the paper in the tin so it goes up the sides.

2 Grate the courgettes (see page 44) using the smaller holes on the grater – you want the courgettes to be grated finely so that they mix into the cake mixture easily.

3 Put the softened butter, sugar and vanilla extract into a bowl and beat with a wooden spoon until creamy. You can also beat with an electric whisk if that is easier.

4 Crack the eggs into a bowl (see page 11). Beat lightly with a fork.

5 Add the eggs gradually to the bowl with the cake batter. Add the milk and whisk together.

6 Put a sieve over your mixing bowl and carefully pour in the flour, baking powder and cocoa powder. Shake the sieve gently so that the ingredients snow down into the bowl. Take a metal spoon and 'fold' into the batter (see Glossary, page 122).

7 Stir in the grated courgettes and mix well.

8 Spoon the cake batter into your tin. Using oven gloves, put the tin in the oven and bake for 35–45 minutes. **Ask an adult to help you** test the centre of the cake with a skewer – when it comes out clean the cake is ready. Leave the cake to cool then cut into squares.

ingredients

3 courgettes (about 450 g), peeled

250 g butter, softened (leave it out of the fridge for ½ hour before you start the recipe)

250 g light brown soft sugar

2 teaspoons vanilla extract

3 eggs

125 ml milk

350 g self-raising flour

1 teaspoon baking powder

4 tablespoons cocoa powder

a cake tin, 30 x 20 cm, greased with butter

makes about 20 squares

peas & beans

  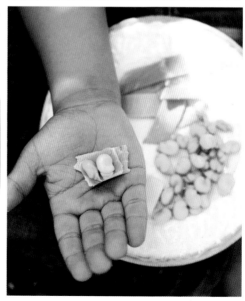

planting peas & beans

Sow from seed

At the beginning of spring the soil should be warm enough to sow pea, broad bean and mangetout seeds straight into the ground. You will then be able to eat your peas and beans in early summer.

If you sow your pea and bean seeds and the weather suddenly turns cold, keep an eye on the seeds and if you don't see any green growth after 10–14 days you may need to sow some more seeds. Cold weather can cause seeds to rot away.

French beans don't like the cold. You will need to sow these seeds at the end of the spring, when the weather is warmer.

1 PREPARE THE SEEDS

I get my children to soak the seeds in a little water for a day before they sow them. The water helps to soften the seeds slightly so that they germinate (see Glossary, page 122) more quickly.

2 CHOOSE A SPACE

Choose a sunny spot that is sheltered and not too windy. Peas and beans like sunshine and because they grow so tall they don't like to be battered by wind.

Peas need to be supported as they are long, spindly plants, so it is ideal if you can plant the seeds along a fence, otherwise you will need to **ask an adult** to make a support for them using canes (pea sticks, see page 84) and string. If you buy a dwarf variety you will not need to do this as they are smaller, bushier plants.

3 PREPARE THE SOIL

Spread a layer of well-rotted manure or your own compost over the soil and have fun digging it into the soil.

Pull out any weeds. It is much easier to keep on top of the weeds if you weed the soil before you sow your seeds.

Sowing peas and mangetout

4 DIG A HOLE

Drag a trowel along the soil to make a small furrow 2.5 cm deep (that's about half a finger!) and 1 cm wide.

5 SOW THE SEEDS

Tip some seeds into your hand, then sow the seeds about 4 cm apart.

6 WATER THE SEEDS

Water the seeds with a special watering can that just sprinkles water gently – if you pour too much water onto the soil in a big gush it might wash the seeds away!

7 SOW MORE SEEDS

Ideally you need to leave about 45 cm in between each row of dwarf peas and 90 cm between each row of taller pea plants so that you have room to get between the plants to pick the peas! If you have the space in your garden, save some seeds for later and sow a few more rows in 2 or 3 weeks' time so that as one crop finishes, your next crop is starting.

Sowing broad beans

Follow steps **1-3** above, then switch to these steps.

4 DIG A HOLE

Dig a hole with your trowel 5 cm deep.

5 SOW THE SEEDS

Pop a seed into the hole and cover with soil. My children pop 2 seeds in each hole in the hope that at least 1 will grow. Leave about 20 cm in between each seed.

6 WATER THE SEEDS

Water the seeds with a special watering can that just sprinkles water gently – if you pour too much water onto the soil in a big gush it might wash the seeds away!

Sowing French beans

For French beans you will need to **ask an adult to help you** make a frame before you begin. A tepee-style frame made of bamboo canes is a fun and easy way to do it. The beans need to have sticks and frames to climb around as they grow.

You can find dwarf varieties of French beans that don't go so high so if you grow these, you won't need to support them.

Follow steps **1-3** above, then switch to these steps.

4 DIG A HOLE

Drag a trowel along the soil to make a small furrow 5 cm deep.

5 SOW THE SEEDS

Put 2 seeds in the hole and cover with soil. If you are growing them tepee-style, sow 2–3 seeds per cane. If you are growing them in a row, sow another 2 seeds with big gaps in between – ideally about 20 cm.

The rows should be about 45 cm apart.

Sowing peas and broad beans inside

You can sow pea and broad bean seeds inside the house – this takes a little effort but it can give your plants a head start.

1 PICK A POT

Find some small pots: plastic cups or cleaned-out yoghurt pots are ideal. **Ask an adult** to poke a few holes in the bottom using a skewer or scissors.

2 ADD SOIL

Three-quarters fill the pot with a general-purpose potting compost.

3 SOW THE SEEDS

Drop 1 seed into each pot. Press gently into the compost and sprinkle a little more compost over the top. Sit the pots on saucers and water. Keep on windowsills.

4 PUT THE POTS OUTSIDE

When the little plants are about 5–8 cm tall, you could put the pots outside for few days to get them used to being outside and then plant them in the ground.

5 PULL OUT A SEEDLING

Prepare the soil just as you would if you were sowing seeds (as above) and then dig a hole. Carefully tip the plant out of the pot and try to keep as much compost around the roots as possible. Put the plant into the hole with its roots facing down. Fill in more soil around the plant, gently press it down with your hands, then water it.

Sowing peas and broad beans outside in pots

You can sow pea and broad bean seeds in a big pot instead of in the garden soil.

1 PICK A POT

Look for a big pot about the size of a bucket (about 30 cm wide at the top). Make sure it has holes in the bottom.

2 ADD SOIL

Three-quarters fill the pot with a general-purpose potting compost. **Ask an adult** to stick 3 canes into the pot and tie them together at the top.

3 SOW THE SEEDS

Push a seed into the compost (about 5 cm deep) next to a cane. Do the same with the other canes. Water gently.

growing peas & beans

Mice love to eat pea seeds so keep an eye on the soil and if you don't see any green shoots after about 10–14 days you might like to sow some more seeds just in case the mice have eaten them!

Make sure that your peas don't get dry and have a good drink of water when they need one.

Whenever you go to check on your peas, gently pull out any weeds that you see growing around the pea plants.

Pea sticks

Ask an adult to help you collect 'pea' sticks – these are needed to support the pea plants when they grow tall and spindly. Any sticks will do but hazel, hornbeam or birch are ideal.

When you, see the green leaves from the seedlings poking through the ground, you can push the sticks into the ground next to them. Wind the seedlings around their nearest cane and they will continue to grow around and up them.

You may need to add some taller pea sticks as the peas grow. They can grow very tall!

If it rains hard or it is very windy the pea plants may fall down if they don't have sticks holding them up.

Broad beans don't normally need any sticks as they are shorter plants.

If you have sown pea seeds outside in pots, 2–3 weeks after sowing, you should see some shoots appear. Twist the stems around the canes as they grow. Water the compost to keep it damp.

Once you can see the bean or pea seedlings it is a good idea to add some straw in between the rows of peas and beans. This helps stop weeds from growing and it also prevents the soil from becoming too dry.

When your plants are flowering

When your broad beans are flowering and you can just see the first pods starting to form at the bottom of the plants, it is a good idea to pick the top 10 cm of the plant. Did you know that this is a special springtime treat? These bits of the plant are called broad bean tips. See page 89 for how to enjoy them!

Spray the flowers with some water to help the pods to grow!

After flowering

When the peas and beans have finished flowering make sure that they have a good watering – this helps the plants to produce lots of yummy beans and peas.

When the beans and peas reach the top of your canes or fence you can pinch the top off the plants to stop them from growing any taller!

Once your plants have lots of beans and pea pods on them you will need to keep picking the pods. If you leave them to get too big the plants will spend all their energy growing these big (less tasty) beans and peas instead of growing more little, sweet peas and beans. See pages 86–87 for more information on picking peas and beans and how to eat them.

Leave a few pods on the plant to dry. You can then pick these pods, open them and inside you should have some slightly dried beans. Put them in an envelope, label them and keep them to grow more bean plants next year.

Slugs and snails

Keep an eye out for slugs and snails and move them off the vegetable patch as soon as you see them – they love bean and pea plants!

If you have a real problem with slugs and snails, you might need to sow some seeds inside and keep them until they are at least 5 cm tall or slightly taller before you plant them. The bigger the plant the better the chance it has of surviving against slugs and snails. When the plants are quite big and have started to wind around the canes you might like to cover the soil with straw to help protect the plants from slugs.

French bean dwarf varieties

Pinch out the tops of the plants (called 'growing tips'). The plants will then start to produce beans instead of growing. This top bit of the plant is also the bit that pests like to eat – it is sweet and sticky and tastes good to them, so if you pinch it off then your plant is more likely to stay healthy.

When the plant has finished producing peas or beans

Ask an adult to cut the plant down, leaving the roots in the soil. The roots are good for the soil. Pop the plant on the compost heap!

harvesting & preparing peas & french beans

Here's a little bit of science for you: once you have taken peas out of their pods the peas will start to lose their sugar as it changes to starch. The main reason that I am telling you this is so that you know why it is a good idea to eat peas on the same day that you have shelled them – they will be sweeter and taste better.

Peas

Take a basket or bowl out into the garden. The pods are ready to pick when they are about 10 cm long.

Make yourself comfortable next to the pea plant. Sit down if you like so that you don't get a sore back from bending down to pick the pea pods. You should be able to break a pea pod away from the plant using your fingers. You might need to pull the pod slightly downwards and twist at the same time so that you pull it away from the stem.

When the peas in their pods are very small, you can eat the whole pod with the peas inside – a bit like mangetout – but I would only eat a few like this. Leave them to get bigger so that you can have fun taking the peas out of the pods and eating them.

'Shelling' is the name given to taking the peas out of their pods. There are a few different ways you might like to do this. You can either snap the pod in half widthways and then you will find it easier to split open each pod half and pick out the peas. Or you might prefer to bend the pod until it splits and then stick your fingers into the split and prise the pod open (see middle picture on the right of this page). Ask a friend to help you so that you can have a chat whilst you work!

You will need about 1½ kg pea pods to have enough shelled peas to feed a family of four.

You don't need to wash peas before eating them because they've been protected from dirt inside their pods. However, watch out for any pods with holes in them because some little maggots might have got inside.

Pea shoots

Have you noticed that there are lots of long tips coming off your pea plant as it grows and climbs (see picture at the top right of this page)? These are the growth tips and the side shoots – normally about 3–4 cm long – and we call them 'pea shoots'. Try one and see if you like it. The Japanese love them so much, they call them 'green gold'. I like adding a few to salads (see page 90) but don't pick too many as the plant needs them to keep producing the pods.

French beans

French beans are ready to harvest when you think they look big enough to eat.

To pick the beans, snap the short stalk that joins the bean to the stem of the plant. Pick a bean and smell it! This may sound silly but it should smell of a fresh bean (unlike many that you buy from the shops!). Try snapping it in half too so that you can see just how fresh it is – it should be crisp. Have you ever eaten French beans that are limp and bendy? Yours should be wonderful and crisp and they should snap easily when you break them.

All you need to prepare French beans is a pair of children's or kitchen scissors (**check with an adult first**) and a bowl. Sit down with a friend and have a chat while you trim. Hold a bean at one end using your thumb and finger. With the other hand snip the other end of the bean. You need to do this with both the stalk end – the end where you pulled the bean away from the stem of the plant – and also the bottom of the bean. Give them a quick rinse under the tap, then they are ready to use.

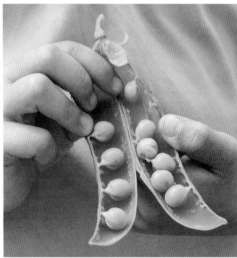

harvesting &
preparing broad beans

Broad beans can be picked at different stages and enjoyed in different ways. Once the pods are ready to pick you will need to keep picking – often 2 or 3 times a week – to encourage the plant to keep producing more pods.

Broad bean tips

Have a look at your broad bean plant and see if you can find any long thin 'tips'. These look a bit like pea shoots (see page 87) and can also be eaten. Pick a few and using scissors snip them into small pieces and add them to a pasta dish like the one on page 98 or just cook them with the beans. Don't take too many as you need them on the plant so that they can keep producing beans.

Picking small pods to enjoy whole

Have you ever eaten a whole broad bean pod with the tiny beans inside? Not many people have. This is really only a treat for gardeners like you who have grown broad beans on your vegetable plot. You can't buy them like this in the shops so it is worth trying them while you can. When the pods are about 5 cm long, pick a few from the plants. You will be able to break the pod away from the plant using your fingers. You might need to pull the pod downwards and twist at the same time so that you pull it away from the stem.

These will need to be prepared just like you would prepare French beans (see page 87). Enjoy them with today's meal – they are best fresh and straight from the garden.

Picking medium–sized pods to enjoy the beans inside

Leave the pods to grow a bit bigger. Harvest the beans by picking the pods from the plant using your fingers. If you find this too hard you might need to use a small pair of scissors but **check with an adult first**. Take a basket or bowl with you to collect the pods in.

You will need about 1½ kg broad bean pods to have enough shelled beans to feed a family of four.

Shelling broad beans

'Shelling' is the name given to taking the beans out of their pods. There are a few different ways you might like to do this. You can either snap the pod in half widthways and then you will find it easier to split open each pod half and pick out the beans. Or you might prefer to bend the pod until it splits and then stick your fingers into the split and prise the pod open. Ask a friend to help you so that you can have a chat whilst you work!

Open a pod and look at the size of the beans (see middle picture on the right of this page). The beans inside the pods should be about the size of your thumbnail. When they are small like this they can be eaten raw.

Picking bigger pods

If you leave the pods on the plant they will carry on growing and get bigger. The beans inside will also get bigger – more like twice the size of your thumbnail.

If the beans are big you might like to slip them out of their skins, which can be great fun (see pictures at the top of the page opposite). Turn to page 92 for instructions on how to 'skin' the beans.

You don't really need to wash beans before eating them because they've been protected from dirt inside their pods. However, watch out for any pods with holes in them because some little maggots might have got inside.

5 ways with peas

Peas are a great snack if you are playing in the garden – you can pick a pod from the plant and eat the peas there and then. Just remember to put the empty pod on the compost heap. There are also lots of things you can do with peas once you get them into the kitchen. My granny always claimed that one of the best ways to cook fresh peas is in their pods. I loved it when she cooked them this way when I was young because I could use my fingers to eat them. Here are 5 ways with peas – try them and see which you like best.

1 PEAS COOKED IN PODS

Quarter-fill a saucepan with water and **ask an adult to help you** turn on the hob. Bring the water to the boil. Pour the peas into the boiling water and set the timer for 3 minutes. **Ask an adult to help you** drain the peas in a colander, then tip them carefully from the colander into a bowl. Dot with butter and watch it melt over the hot pods. Everyone can pick up a pod from its stem end and suck the little peas out of the pod.

2 PEA SHOOT SALAD

Choose some fresh salad – if you have any that you have grown, use those but if not, buy some. Wash the leaves. Pick some pea shoots from your pea plants with some of their leaves and scatter them over the salad. You don't need too many as they have a strong flavour and you should also leave lots of shoots on the plant to produce more peas. Make your favourite dressing and drizzle it over the top of the salad.

3 BOILED PEAS

Quarter-fill a saucepan with water. Put the shelled peas and a sprig or two of fresh mint into it. Cover the pan with a lid and **ask an adult to help you** turn on the hob. Cook for 2 minutes (for small, fresh peas) or 3 minutes (for bigger, older peas) until just cooked. They will be tender but still have a little bite. **Ask an adult to help you** drain the peas in a colander. They're ready to eat!

4 FREEZING PEAS

Fill a big bowl with really cold water and set it to one side. Quarter-fill a saucepan with water and **ask an adult to help you** turn on the hob. Bring the water to the boil. Pour the peas into the boiling water and set the timer for 2 minutes. This is called 'blanching' (see Glossary, page 122). **Ask an adult to help you** drain the peas in a colander, then tip them from the colander into the bowl of cold water to stop them cooking any more. Drain, put into freezer bags and freeze for up to a few months.

5 STEAMED PEAS

Half-fill a saucepan with water. Put the peas into a colander or steamer inside the pan (the bottom of the colander/steamer should be above the water). Put the lid on the pan. **Ask an adult to help you** turn on the hob. Bring the water to the boil, then steam the peas for 2 minutes (for small, fresh peas) or 3 minutes (for bigger, older peas).

cooking with peas & beans

5 ways with beans

My son refused to eat broad beans until we started to grow them. He didn't like the taste or texture. When we picked some small of our small broad beans, cooked them and ate them with freshly cooked pasta – he loved them. He even tried one raw when we were preparing them in the kitchen and liked it so much that the following day we all had some raw broad beans with ham and cheese for lunch. Try some of these easy ways to eat beans and see which you like best.

5 WAYS

1 RAW BROAD BEANS WITH HAM & CHEESE

If your beans are small, about the size of your thumbnail, you might like to eat them raw. Try one and see if you like it. If you do like the texture and flavour, you might like to try this: pile a few fresh, raw beans onto a plate. Using the 'bridge' cutting technique (see page 11), slice a piece of cheese and add this to the plate. Chop a couple of slices of cooked ham too, and then all you need is a piece of bread or some boiled new potatoes (see page 42) and you have a complete meal.

2 SKINNING BIG BROAD BEANS

If your beans are much bigger than a thumbnail, you might like to take them out of their 'skins' before you eat them. Quarter-fill a saucepan with water and **ask an adult to help you** turn on the hob. Bring the water to the boil. Pour the beans into the boiling water and cook for 5 minutes. **Ask an adult to help you** drain the peas in a colander, then leave until cool enough to pick up. Hold one between your thumb and one finger and pinch it to squeeze it out of its skin – the bright green bean should pop out.

3 FREEZING BROAD BEANS

Fill a big bowl with really cold water and set it to one side. Quarter-fill a saucepan with water and **ask an adult to help you** turn on the hob. Bring the water to the boil. Pour the beans into the boiling water and set the timer for 2 minutes. This is called 'blanching' (see Glossary, page 122). **Ask an adult to help you** drain the beans in a colander, then tip them carefully from the colander into the bowl of cold water to stop them cooking any more. Drain, put into freezer bags and freeze.

4 BOILED FRENCH BEANS & DIP

Half-fill a saucepan with water and **ask an adult to help you** turn on the hob. Bring the water to the boil. Pour the beans into the boiling water and cook (without a lid on the pan) for 5 minutes. **Ask an adult to help you** fish a bean out to taste it – it should still have some crunch. **Ask an adult to help you** drain the beans in a colander, then tip them carefully from the colander into a bowl. Mix together an equal amount of mayonnaise and natural yoghurt. Using scissors, snip some fresh chives and stir into the dip, then serve with the beans.

5 STEAMED & DRESSED FRENCH BEANS

Put 1 peeled and crushed clove of garlic, the juice of 1 lemon and 3 tablespoons olive oil in a jug and mix. Taste and add more oil or some honey if you think it needs sweetening. Half-fill a saucepan with water. Put some trimmed French beans into a colander or steamer inside the pan (the bottom of the colander/steamer should be above the water). Put the lid on the pan. **Ask an adult to help you** turn on the hob. Bring the water to the boil, then steam the beans for 3–4 minutes. Pour the dressing over the top.

pea, bean & new potato salad

If you want to make this salad even more delicious and a bit fancy, you could try adding tinned tuna, olives and tomatoes to it to make it more like a French 'salade Niçoise'.

1 Boil the new potatoes (see page 42).

2 To hard-boil the eggs, half-fill a saucepan with water and **ask an adult to help you** turn on the hob. Bring the water to the boil. Using a spoon, gently lower each egg into the boiling water and set the timer for 7 minutes.

3 **Ask an adult to help you** drain the eggs in a colander in the sink, then pour cold water over them to cool them down. When the eggs are really cold, peel off their shells. Using the 'bridge' cutting technique (see page 11), cut the eggs into quarters.

4 Boil the peas and French beans (see pages 91 and 93). Put in a big salad bowl with the potatoes, eggs and lettuce.

5 Mix together the olive oil and vinegar, add to the salad and gently mix together.

ingredients

450 g new potatoes

4 eggs

4 handfuls of fresh, shelled peas

about 200 g French beans, trimmed

a few handfuls of lettuce leaves

2 tablespoons olive oil

2 teaspoons red wine or cider vinegar

makes enough for 4

COOK IT

pea purée bruschetta

You can make this purée with broad beans instead of peas but it is probably best to skin them before you purée them. Look at page 92 for instructions on how to skin broad beans.

ingredients

about 150 g shelled peas (or skinned broad beans)

1 lemon, washed

3 tablespoons olive oil

½ clove of garlic, peeled

a handful of fresh mint leaves

about 8 slices of French bread

makes enough for 4

1 Boil the peas (see page 91).

2 Using a cheese grater, grate the lemon – use the smaller holes on the grater so that you get very small shreds of lemon skin (called 'zest'). Try not to grate any of the white bit under the skin, called the 'pith', as this is bitter and not nice to eat. Grate the zest straight into a food processor.

3 Now using the 'bridge' cutting technique (see page 11), cut the lemon in half and squeeze out the juice into the food processor.

4 Add the peas, olive oil, garlic and mint into the food processor and **ask an adult to help you** blend until you get a smooth purée.

5 **Ask an adult to help you** toast the bread slices in a toaster or under a hot grill, then spread the pea purée on the toast. You can add some more fresh mint leaves on top if you like.

pasta with french beans & pesto

If your parents are ever stuck for an idea for supper, why don't you suggest that you help make this pasta dish – it is quick and you only need a few ingredients.

1 Fill a big saucepan with water, put on the hob and **ask an adult to help you** turn on the heat. Bring to the boil, then **ask an adult to help you** add the pasta and look at the pack instructions for how long to cook it.

2 Two minutes before the pasta has finished cooking, add the beans to the pasta pan and cook.

3 Ask an adult to help you drain the pasta and beans and tip them back into the empty pan.

4 Add the pesto and carefully stir to coat the pasta with the pesto. Season with freshly ground black pepper. Sprinkle the cheese over the top and serve.

ingredients

about 400 g pasta of your choice or as much as you think your family will eat

200 g French beans, snapped in half if they are very long

4 tablespoons home-made pesto (see page 28) or shop-bought pesto

freshly ground black pepper

75 g grated Parmesan cheese

makes enough for 4

COOK IT

pasta with broad beans & bacon

Broad beans taste delicious mixed with a lightly smoked bacon and grated cheese. My eldest daughter Ella says this is one of the easiest pasta sauces you can make. She also makes it with fresh peas.

1 Using a rolling pin slightly squash the clove of garlic. This will help to release the garlicky flavour into the sauce.

2 Ask an adult to help you put a heavy-based saucepan or deep frying pan on the hob over high heat. Add the bacon bits and fry for 1 minute. Turn the heat down, add the clove of garlic and fry, stirring with a wooden spoon, until the bacon is cooked and just beginning to go slightly crisp.

3 Add the double cream and stir. Turn off the heat and leave to one side.

4 Fill a big saucepan with water, put on the hob and ask an adult to help you turn on the heat. Bring to the boil, then ask an adult to help you add the pasta and look at the pack instructions for how long to cook it.

5 Four minutes before the pasta has finished cooking, add the broad beans to the pasta pan and cook.

6 Ask an adult to help you drain the pasta and beans and tip them back into the empty pasta pan.

7 Taste the sauce and add the fresh herbs. Season with freshly ground black pepper.

8 Add the sauce to the pan with the cooked pasta and broad beans. Ask an adult to help you heat it up gently over low heat until warmed through, mixing with a wooden spoon.

9 Sprinkle the cheese over the top and serve.

COOK IT

ingredients

1 clove of garlic, peeled

200 g good-quality chopped bacon – look out for lardons or pancetta cubes (this is slightly smoked and tastes delicious)

170 ml double cream

about 350 g shelled broad beans or peas

about 400 g pasta of your choice or as much as you think your family will eat (this sauce works really well with spaghetti or linguine)

fresh basil leaves or mint, snipped with scissors

freshly ground black pepper

grated Parmesan cheese, to serve

makes enough for 4

strawberries
& raspberries

planting strawberries

Strawberries grow well in raised beds or pots outside. It's easiest to grow strawberries from seedlings/plug plants (not seeds), which you can find in your local garden centre.

When to sow the plants

Plant small strawberry plants in the spring. The plants will only grow a few fruit during the first year but you will have more fruit next year.

Choose your strawberries

There are so many different plants to choose from. If you are not sure which type to choose, you might like to try a couple to see which do well in your garden. If you're lucky they will produce fruit all through the summer so that you have a constant supply (they may not, but it is worth a go!).

Alpine strawberries are much smaller than the normal strawberries that you see in the shops.

Planting in the garden

Ideally about 2 hours before you start the gardening, water your plant in its pot.

1 CHOOSE A SPACE

Choose a sunny spot in the garden.

2 PREPARE THE SOIL

Spread a layer of well-rotted manure or your own compost over the soil and have fun digging it into the soil.

3 DIG A HOLE

Dig a hole with your trowel in the soil.

4 TIP THE PLANT OUT

Carefully tip the plant out of the pot and try to keep as much compost around the roots as possible. Put the plant into the hole with its roots facing down.

5 TUCK THE PLANT IN

Fill in more soil around the plant, gently press it down with your hands, then give it a good drink of water. Pull off any fruit that is already growing to encourage the plant to grow more fruit.

In a raised bed you can plant the plants about 30 cm apart. In a big garden you might want to leave more space around the plants so that they have more room to grow and so that you have room to get between the plants to pick the fruit.

Planting in pots

1 PICK A POT

Look for a big pot about the size of a bucket (about 30 cm wide at the top) with holes in the bottom. Put some broken bits of pots, pebbles or shells into the bottom.

2 CHOOSE A SPACE

Choose a sunny, sheltered spot for the pot (against a south-facing wall is ideal – ask your parents where they think is best).

3 ADD SOIL

Three-quarters fill the pot with a general-purpose potting compost and use your trowel to dig a little hole in the centre of the compost for the plant.

4 TIP THE PLANT OUT

Carefully tip the plant out of the pot and try to keep as much compost around the roots as possible. Put the plant into the hole with its roots facing down.

5 TUCK THE PLANT IN

Fill in more soil around the plant, gently press it down with your hands, then give it a good drink of water.

planting & growing raspberries

Planting autumn raspberries

Autumn raspberries are easier to grow than summer raspberries – they don't need as much space and they are easier to look after. Plus they come into fruit as the strawberries have stopped. Hopefully you will have ripe berries to pick from the end of the summer and they may keep going until the end of the winter. Unlike strawberries, raspberries can only be grown in the ground, not in pots.

The great thing about raspberries is that they can carry on producing fruit year after year. My granddad had raspberry plants that produced fruit for more than 25 years!

Ideally about 2 hours before you start the gardening, water your plant in its pot.

1 CHOOSE A SPACE

Choose a sunny, sheltered spot.

2 PREPARE THE SOIL

Spread a layer of well-rotted manure or your own compost over the soil and have fun digging it into the soil.

3 DIG A HOLE

Dig a hole with your trowel in the soil.

4 TIP THE PLANT OUT

Carefully tip the plant out of the pot and try to keep as much compost around the roots as possible. Put the plant into the hole with its roots facing down.

5 TUCK THE PLANT IN

Fill in more soil around the plant, gently press it down with your hands, then give it a good drink of water.

6 PLANT MORE PLANTS

Plant in rows with at least 30 cm in between them so you can get between the plants to pick the fruit.

Growing

Look at the raspberry plant on the top left of this page. Can you see the pretty flower? In the middle of the flower is a tiny green raspberry fruit. It will need lots more sun and rain before the fruit is ripe and juicy.

When you haven't had any rain try to remember to water your raspberry 'canes' (the roots of the raspberry plant). If the plants get too dry they will only produce a few small fruit. They need water to help produce lots of fruit.

Watch out for the birds!

Birds love raspberries! If you have some netting it is probably safest to put it over the plant as soon you see fruits coming through just in case the birds try to get at them. **Ask an adult to help you.** You can buy netting from a garden centre.

You will just need to **remind adults** to cut your autumn raspberry canes back to ground level at the end of the winter, ready to start growing again the following year.

growing strawberries

Like raspberries, strawberries grow from the middle of the plant's flowers.

Strawberry plants normally come into flower around the end of the springtime.

The middle, yellow bit of the flower is called the 'stamen'. This changes to a small green fruit (see picture on the top right of this page). This green fruit gradually gets bigger and bigger and will eventually turn into a beautiful red strawberry (see pictures on the middle and bottom right of this page). I think this is amazing, don't you?

When you see just how many flowers there are on your strawberry plants it is hard not to get too excited about how many fruits you will be able to eat in a month's time! But you need to keep looking after your plant to help make sure that it will have lots of fresh fruit for you.

If you have some straw you can put this around the plants to stop the strawberry fruits from touching the soil or getting splashed with mud.

Pull out weeds whenever you see them appear around the strawberry plant.

It is really important to keep watering strawberry plants, especially if they are in pots or hanging baskets. This is particularly important if the weather is hot and dry. Strawberry plants in pots will suffer quite quickly if they dry out.

Watch out for the birds!
Birds love strawberries as well as raspberries! If you have some netting it is probably safest to put it over the plant as

soon you see fruits coming through just in case the birds try to get at them. **Ask an adult to help you**. You can buy netting from a garden centre.

Runners and plantlets
If the plants are healthy they should start to produce 'runners' (see Glossary, page 122) and make 'plantlets' (little plants) which will root themselves around their 'mother' plant. If there is room around the mother plants for these plantlets, then leave them where they are. If you are short of space you may need to cut the runner, gently dig up the plantlet and plant it in a new position in the garden.

When the new little plantlets start to grow roots you can cut them away from the 'mummy' plant, but leave at least 5 cm of the runner attached to the plant. Plant the new plant and then look after them in the same way as you did the other plants.

When the plants have finished growing fruit
Ask an adult to help you cut all the old leaves off the plants, leaving a few centimetres of the stalk and then spread some more well-rotted manure or compost around the plants.

Alpine strawberries
The middle picture on the right of this page shows an alpine strawberry plant (see also top left and right pictures on page 101). These produce small, more delicately flavoured strawberries. These tend to be tougher than conventional strawberries and very easy to grow.

harvesting & preparing strawberries & raspberries

Even though it is VERY tempting to pick strawberries
and raspberries as soon as they are red, try to resist them
for a day or two longer. This will give the fruit a chance
to turn from red to a deeper red and at the same time
they will become sweeter, juicier and have a stronger
flavour. It is worth the wait!

Strawberries

I find that the number of strawberries in a bowl for a meal varies depending on who is doing the picking! (I am sure my son Finley, who is 6 years old, picks one for the bowl and then one for him, one for the bowl and then one for him...). Always try to hold the stalk instead of the fruit when you are picking – this way you are less likely to squash or damage the strawberry. Hold the stalk with your finger and thumb and break it off the plant – it should snap quite easily. Try not to pull the plant as you pick the fruit otherwise you may pull the whole plant out of the ground. Strawberry plants are low to the ground so you will be more comfortable sitting down if you plan to pick a lot of fruit.

Once you have started to pick your strawberries you will need to check the plants every day and keep picking any that are ripe and ready. You don't want them to stay on the plant for too long as they can start to go really soft and squishy. However, if you do find some fruit that has already started to go quite soft, pick it and add it to a smoothie. If you find fruit that has started to go mouldy, pick it and put it on the compost heap. If it stays on the plant it may cause some of the other fruit to go mouldy, too.

Hulling strawberries

To 'hull' a strawberry simply means to remove the green leaves and the stalk. The easiest way to do this is to pick them off with your fingers but you will need to make sure that you pull out the hard bit where the fruit and the stalk meet.

You may see adults using a knife to hull the strawberry, but if you do it this way you tend to lose the lovely shape of the fruit as you cut its top off.

Washing

You don't have to wash strawberries, unless there is dirt on them. If they are dirty fill a bowl of cold water, put the strawberries into the bowl and then take them out and drain them in a colander. Try not to leave strawberries sitting in water for too long as they can start to taste watery.

If you want to cut the fruit before you serve it, see page 109 and the picture on the bottom right of this page.

Picking raspberries

When my children go outside to pick the raspberries this is the only time that I ask them to wash their hands before they go into the garden! This is because you don't want to wash the fruit once you have picked it: raspberries are so delicate that washing them can damage their texture and flavour.

Pull the raspberry carefully away from the stalk, leaving the core of the fruit still attached to the plant. This is quite different to when you pick strawberries as some of the stalk and leaves will still be attached to the strawberry fruit (see above). Put the raspberries straight into the bowl that you want to serve them from!

Pick over raspberries just removing any leaves or stalk and they are ready to eat.

If you would be happier giving them a wash before you eat them fill a bowl with cold water and put the berries into the water. Take them out and leave them to drain on kitchen paper.

5 ways with strawberries

Try to resist eating too many strawberries when you are picking them so that you can enjoy making a few different treats with the fruit. Strawberry lollies are easy to make but you do need to be patient while you wait for them to freeze. Something slightly more instant is a quick and easy strawberry fool, ideal on a warm summer's day. If you are fortunate enough to have too many strawberries to know what to do with them, purée the fruit and freeze the purée. You can use it to drizzle over ice cream or cakes. Whole, fresh strawberries don't freeze very well so it's best to purée them with a little sugar first.

1 STRAWBERRY ICE CUBES

Using a fork or potato masher, mash some hulled, ripe strawberries in a bowl until smooth. Add a little orange juice and mix together. Put pieces of chopped strawberry into an ice cube tray. Pour the strawberry and orange juice mixture into the tray on top of the strawberry pieces and freeze. When frozen put a couple of the cubes into a glass of water or lemonade. The cubes will give your drink a hint of strawberry flavour.

2 STRAWBERRY FOOL

Using a fork or potato masher, mash 250 g hulled, ripe strawberries in a bowl until smooth. Add 500 ml Greek yoghurt and 2 teaspoons runny honey and very gently mix everything together until smooth. Spoon into small bowls or glasses and put into the fridge for at least 10 minutes before serving.

3 STRAWBERRY SALAD

Hull a big bowl of strawberries, then follow the instructions for how to chop strawberries on this page. Put the pieces into a bowl. Squeeze some fresh orange juice over the top – not too much, but just enough so that the juice comes halfway up the bowl. Sprinkle a little icing sugar or caster sugar over the top and if you have some fresh mint, pick a few leaves and pop them on the top too.

4 STRAWBERRY PUREE

Ask an adult to help you use a food processor or blender for this purée and remember that the blade in the middle is as sharp as a knife – don't touch it! Put 450 g hulled strawberries and 3 tablespoons golden caster sugar into the processor or blender and whiz until smooth. Pour into small containers that can go into the freezer. Write the date on a sticky label and stick to the container. It will keep in the freezer for a few months. When you need to use it, leave it out to melt.

5 HOW TO CHOP STRAWBERRIES

Take a hulled strawberry. Using the 'bridge' cutting technique (see page 11), cut the strawberry in half. Rest the cut side of the strawberry on the chopping board and using the 'bridge' cutting technique again, cut the strawberry half in half again to make quarters.

5 ways with raspberries

In my family, we struggle to make too many things with our raspberries because we all love eating them just as they are. However, when they do make it to the kitchen, these are some of our favourite ways to use them. Lola, my middle daughter, loves to make raspberry ice cubes to add to summer drinks whereas Ella, my eldest, is happier making a berry salad in a really big bowl with a big serving spoon – ready for everyone to help themselves.

1 BERRY FRUIT SALAD

This is a great way of practising some of the skills that you have learnt so far, for example hulling strawberries and chopping fruit. Put a big handful of hulled strawberries into a bowl. Add 2 big handfuls of fresh raspberries. Add any other berries or fruit that you have. Squeeze some fresh orange juice over the top. Using scissors, cut some fresh mint into small pieces and sprinkle over the top. This is delicious with the Raspberry and Lemon Ice Cream on page 117.

2 FREEZING RASPBERRIES

If you are lucky enough to have lots of raspberries on your canes, you might like to try freezing some. They freeze well just as they are (unlike strawberries). Find a plastic lid or small tray that will fit in the freezer. Put the raspberries in a single layer on the tray and put it in the freezer. If you pile the fruit on top of each other they will stick together when they freeze and you won't be able to separate them easily. Once they are frozen, put a handful of them into freezer bags. Write the date on a sticky label and stick to the bags.

3 RASPBERRY MILKSHAKE

Ask an adult to help you use a food processor or blender for this milkshake and remember that the blade in the middle is as sharp as a knife – don't touch it! Put 2 handfuls of raspberries in the processor or blender and pour in 2 glasses of fresh milk. Blend until you have a pink milkshake. You might like to add a little honey if it is not sweet enough, or a scoop of ice cream as a treat. Pour into 2 glasses.

4 RASPBERRY ICE CUBES

My children love making these. Just put a fresh raspberry into each ice cube tray compartment, then cover with apple juice or water and freeze. These look pretty in any drink on a warm day.

5 RASPBERRY DIP WITH BANANAS

Using a fork or potato masher, mash some raspberries in a bowl until quite smooth and a bit runny. Taste and if it is not sweet enough for your liking, add a teaspoon of icing sugar. Spoon into a little bowl. Peel some bananas and using the 'bridge' cutting technique (see page 11), cut into big pieces for dipping into the dip.

mini strawberry cakes

Before you make these cakes make sure that you leave the butter out of the fridge until it is soft – it will make it much easier to mix the butter and sugar together. This is called 'creaming'.

1 Turn the oven on to 180°C (350°F) Gas 4. Put 12 paper cases into a cupcake tray.

2 Cream the softened butter, sugar and vanilla extract with a wooden spoon until the butter is soft and creamy and pale in colour (see page 11 for instructions on how to 'cream').

3 Crack the eggs into a bowl (see page 11). Beat lightly with a fork.

4 Add a little egg to the creamed butter mixture and beat with the wooden spoon. Add a little more egg and beat again. Keep doing this until you have added all the eggs.

5 You can add a little flour if the mixture looks as though it is starting to separate.

6 Put a sieve over your mixing bowl and carefully pour in the flour. Shake the sieve gently so that the flour snows down into the bowl. Take a metal spoon and 'fold' (see Glossary, page 122) into the batter.

7 Add a little milk – just enough so that the mixture softens enough to drop easily from the spoon – this is called 'dropping consistency'.

8 Spoon the mixture into the paper cases until each one is about is two-thirds full. Using your oven gloves, put the cakes into the hot oven and bake for 13–15 minutes until risen and

golden and the cakes are springy to touch. **Ask an adult to help you** take the cupcake tray out of the oven and leave to cool a little. Then put the cupcakes on a cooling rack to cool down while you make the icing.

9 To make the icing, mash the strawberries in a big bowl with a fork, add the icing sugar and mix until quite smooth. Spoon the icing onto the cakes and top with chopped or whole strawberries. You may need to add a little liquid depending on how juicy the strawberries are. You can either add another strawberry, which will make the icing a stronger pink colour, or you can just add a few drops of water.

COOK IT

ingredients

175 g butter, softened (leave it out of
the fridge for about ½ hour before you
start the recipe)

175 g golden caster sugar

a few drops of vanilla extract

3 eggs

175 g self-raising flour

2 tablespoons milk

for the icing

2 ripe, juicy fresh strawberries

175 g icing sugar

a handful of fresh strawberries,
to decorate

a cupcake tray and 12 paper cases

makes about 12 mini cakes

strawberry eton mess

This is great for practising whisking, but if you use a hand whisk you may need to pass the whisk around so that your arm doesn't get too tried! If you use an electric whisk, **you will need an adult to help you.**

1 Follow the instructions on page 109 for chopping the strawberries. Cut them in halves or quarters – whatever you prefer.

2 Put the cream into a large bowl and using a hand whisk or an electric whisk (**with the help of an adult**), whisk until it makes soft peaks. This means that when you lift up the whisk the cream shapes itself into soft peaks. Don't over-whisk otherwise the cream will be too firm.

3 Add the yoghurt and gently 'fold' everything together with a spoon. Hold a meringue over another bowl and gently crush with your fingers to break into small pieces.

4 Add the meringue pieces and strawberries to the cream mixture and gently mix together.

5 Spoon the mixture into small bowls and put in the fridge for 20 minutes before you serve.

ingredients

16 ripe, juicy strawberries

300 ml double (or whipping) cream

200 g thick Greek-style yoghurt

6 plain meringues or meringue shells

makes enough for 4–6

COOK IT

raspberry smoothie lollies

Have you ever made anything that needs to be frozen before you can eat it? Most food contains lots of water. Freezing works by changing this water to ice.

ingredients

2 ripe bananas
250 g raspberries
about 300 ml milk

makes about 6 lollies

1 Before you start making your own lollies you will need to find something to make them in. If you don't have 6 shop-bought lolly moulds, don't worry – use egg cups or empty yoghurt pots instead. You can buy wooden lolly sticks from the shops but if you can't find any use a plastic spoon instead. Don't use metal spoons as these will be too cold to hold when they come out of the freezer.

2 First, fill your moulds with water. Then pour the water from the moulds into a measuring jug. Read the total amount on the side of the jug and write it down.

3 Peel the bananas and break them into pieces. Put them into a food processor or blender with the raspberries and **ask an adult to help you** whiz until smooth.

4 Carefully pour this mixture into the measuring jug, then top up with enough milk to make it up to the measurement you made wrote down earlier. Pour into the lolly moulds. Fill the moulds almost, but not quite, to the top. When liquid freezes, it expands. This is because water particles get bigger when they turn to ice. so it is important that you leave a small gap at the top of the mould so that the liquid can expand.

5 Put into the freezer for at least 3–4 hours.

6 When it is time to eat the lollies you may need to dip the mould into hot water for just a minute to help the lolly slide out but don't leave it sitting in hot water for very long or the lolly will melt!

chocolate-dipped strawberries

This is a great recipe for practising melting chocolate. Once you have learnt how to melt chocolate, there are so many things that you can do with it, like drizzling it over cakes.

1 Find a bowl that will sit on top of a saucepan, so that the bottom of the bowl is just under the rim of the pan.

2 Half-fill the saucepan with water and **ask an adult to help you** turn on the hob. Bring the water to a gentle 'simmer' (see Glossary, page 122).

3 Put the chocolate pieces in the bowl you have found and **ask an adult** to rest the bowl of chocolate in the pan so it sits above the simmering water but does not touch it. Leave it for 1 minute.

4 **Ask an adult to help you** remove the pan from the hob. Stir the chocolate gently until it

has melted but don't let it get too hot otherwise the cocoa butter will begin to separate from the cocoa solids. The solids will burn if the chocolate is overheated and the chocolate will become dry and crumbly.

5 Hold a strawberry by its stalk and half dip it into the chocolate. Rest on a plate and leave to set.

6 It is really important that you do not let any liquid like water drip into the chocolate because even a tiny amount can cause the chocolate to become hard and turn into a solid lump!

ingredients

1 bar of good-quality milk chocolate, broken up into small, evenly sized pieces

a few handfuls of ripe strawberries

makes lots!

raspberry & lemon ice cream

You need to be patient with this recipe – it will need to freeze overnight – but it is worth the wait, or at least that's what the children who tested this recipe told me!

1 Using a fork or potato masher, mash the raspberries in a big bowl. Add the lemon curd and yoghurt and carefully mix everything together with a spoon.

2 Put the cream into a large bowl and using a hand whisk or an electric whisk (**with the help of an adult**), whisk until it makes soft peaks. This means that when you lift up the whisk the cream shapes itself into soft peaks. Don't over-whisk otherwise the cream will be too firm.

3 Gently fold the cream into the raspberry and lemon curd mixture.

4 Pour into a freezerproof container or wash out an ice cream tub and use that. Cover with a tight-fitting lid and freeze for about 6 hours. You will need to take it out of the freezer for 5–10 minutes before you want to eat it so that

ingredients

250 g raspberries

325 g lemon curd
(most jars are about this size)

500 g thick Greek yoghurt
(do try to find the Greek or
Greek-style yoghurt as this has
a wonderful creamy texture)

284 ml (a tub) whipping cream

makes enough for about 6

easy things to grow in your kitchen

How to grow mustard & cress

It is fun growing food in your kitchen. Have you ever grown cress? It is very simple and the cress seeds will grow very quickly, if you start now you should have some cress to eat within a week.

You can try growing a pot of mustard seeds and a pot of cress seeds at the same time so that you end up with mustard and cress in your sandwich or in your salad. The picture on the opposite page, bottom right, is of some lovely mustard.

This is what you'll need:

Pot: For growing your cress in, for example a cardboard fruit or vegetable pot, or a yoghurt pot or an ice cream tub.

Kitchen paper or cotton wool: Enough to cover the bottom of your pot.

A packet of seeds: Cress, mustard, alfalfa, radish or beetroot seeds.

Water: To provide moisture for the seeds.

First, clean the pot that you are going to grow your cress in.

Soak the kitchen paper or cotton wool in water until it feels damp to the touch. Put the damp kitchen paper or cotton wool in the bottom of the pot. Sprinkle some cress seeds into the pot and then put it in a warm place. Keep checking your cress each day and within about 7 days you should have a pot full of cress!

How to sprout seeds

Did you know that when a seed is covered with water, it sucks the water in, swells and splits open? It then sends roots down into the soil and pushes the shoots up and out into the garden. This is how a plant starts to grow.

Sometimes we can eat seeds without planting them in the ground. We can make them swell and sprout shoots and then eat them in a sandwich or in a salad. They taste crunchy and delicious.

This is what you'll need:

A few old jam jars: You will need a jam jar for each different type of seed.

Seeds: For example, chickpeas, brown lentils, red lentils and mung beans – go to a health food shop and ask the shop assistant if he or she has anything suitable for sprouting at home.

Tepid water: This means slightly warm or lukewarm, not cold. You can make the water tepid by pouring cold water into a jug and then adding a little hot water. When you dip your finger into the jug the water should be like your body – not cold and not hot.

Some thin fabric: You want cotton or muslin, to cover your jars with.

Some rubber bands: For stretching over the fabric covering your jars.

First, clean the jars that you are going to sprout your seeds in.

Put a handful of seeds in a jar and fill the jar with tepid water.

Stretch a piece of fabric over the jar and hold it tight with a rubber band.

Put the jar on your windowsill and leave overnight.

In the picture on the opposite page, top left, you will see 2 jars with seeds that haven't yet sprouted: radish seeds on the left and alfalfa seeds on the right.

The next day, remove the fabric covering and carefully drain away the water, making sure you don't lose any seeds. Transfer the seeds to a dish while you rinse out the jar.

Put the seeds back in the jar and pour in a little tepid water – just enough to cover the seeds. Put the jar on your windowsill and leave overnight.

The next day, drain the water and just cover with tepid water again. Keep doing this every day until the seeds have sprouted (see picture opposite, top right). Alfalfa seeds are quite quick to grow – they take about 3 days. Other seeds may take a bit longer.

Quick sandwich idea

1 Using a pair of kitchen scissors, snip some of your home-grown mustard and cress at the bottom of their stems.

2 Spread some hummous onto a slice of bread, top with grated carrot and then sprinkle over the mustard and cress.

3 Cover with another slice of bread and cut the sandwich in half. The mustard and cress add a little flavour and texture.

growing edible flowers

Always check with an adult before you eat anything that is growing in your garden. Sometimes flowers can be eaten, like nasturtiums, lavender, marigold flowers, chives, thyme, rose petals and courgette flowers but it's best to check first.

They are easy to grow so if you don't already have them growing in your garden, try planting some to use when cooking.

How to grow nasturtiums

Nasturtium flowers have lovely big seeds that are easy to plant and they can be planted straight in the ground. They look really pretty growing alongside a garden path or grown in a pot (see picture opposite, bottom left).

To plant in the ground, pull out any weeds first and then rake the top of the soil to break up any lumps. Nasturtiums don't need any compost.

Sow the seeds following the packet instructions. Normally you need to push the seed into the ground about 2 cm deep and leave about 10 cm in between each seed to allow room for the flowers to grow.

Water the seeds with a special watering can that just sprinkles water gently – if you pour too much water onto the soil in a big gush it might wash the seeds away!

Leave them until they have germinated – you should be able to see a little green shoot after 7–10 days.

Keep watering the plants as they grow and when you have some pretty flowers on your plant, pick the flowers. If you keep picking the flowers, more of them will keep appearing for you to pick! Nasturtiums often have bright, tropical-looking flowers that range in colour from bright yellow and orange to red, but there are also some varieties that grow pale flowers like pink and cream.

A few things to try with edible flowers

Try sprinkling nasturtium flowers or marigold petals over salads – they have a lovely peppery flavour.

My girls love making crystallized rose petals. They whip a little egg white with a fork and then lightly brush it all over rose petals, then sprinkle the petals with caster sugar and leave to dry in an airing cupboard. These look really pretty scattered on top of cakes.

To separate an egg, crack the egg following the instructions on page 11 but crack it onto a saucer instead of a bowl. Put a small round biscuit cutter over the yolk (big enough not to touch the yolk so that the yolk doesn't split) and gently tip the white off the saucer into a bowl. You can now gently whisk the egg white with a fork.

Sprinkle chive flowers over salads or cooked green vegetables to add a little hint of onion flavour.

Lavender plants

Buy a small lavender plant and put it into the ground, water it and watch it grow. The pretty lilac flowers (see pictures opposite, top left and right) have a great scent and taste good in biscuits like these shortbreads.

Lavender shortbread biscuits

125 g butter, softened (leave it out of the fridge for about ½ hour before you start the recipe)

55 g golden caster sugar

3 teaspoons lavender flowers

180 g plain flour

2 baking trays, greased with a little butter

a biscuit cutter, about 5 cm across

makes about 25 shortbread biscuits

1 Pick the little purple lavender flowers out of the stem leaving the hard stem behind. You can do this by rubbing your fingers down the flowers or by carefully pulling the flowers out away from the stem. You can use dried lavender buds instead of the fresh, open flowers but in this case you will need only 2 teaspoons because the flavour is stronger.

2 Turn the oven on to 180°C (350°F) Gas 4.

3 Cream the softened butter, sugar and lavender flowers with a wooden spoon until the butter is soft and creamy and pale in colour (see page 11 about 'creaming').

4 Add the flour and stir until you have a smooth paste.

5 Sprinkle some flour over a clean work surface and then put the dough on the table. Break the dough in half. Sprinkle some flour over a rolling pin and then roll out one half of the dough until it is about 1 cm thick.

6 Using the biscuit cutter, cut out circles from the dough. Lift the circles of dough onto the baking trays – you might need to use a flat spatula or palette knife to do this.

7 Using oven gloves, put the trays into the hot oven and bake for 12 minutes – when they are ready they should be golden around the edges. If they are not, **ask an adult to help you** put them back into the oven for another 2 minutes.

glossary

Here are a few useful gardening and cooking words you might come across when you are looking through the book.

GARDENING

Annual: Used to describe a plant that only lives for one year. You will need to plant another one next year.

Claggy: Soil that is heavy and sticky, not suitable for growing.

Companion planting: Plants are sometimes happier when they are near another type of plant. Some plants can help others by providing nutrients for the soil. They can also offer protection from the sun or wind or stop pests from eating the plants. For example, carrots and onions like to be near each other.

Cut-and-come-again leaves: Salad leaves that grow back after you have picked them. Just make sure that you leave at least 3 cm of leaf when you pick the leaves to allow for re-growth.

Earthing up: Earthing up potatoes is an important part of the growing process. It involves piling soil up and around the plant to stop new tubers from turning green and then poisonous. Sometimes this is called 'hilling'.

Furrow: A long, narrow, shallow hole made in the soil. In a big field, a farmer would use a plough to do this but in a small area you can make a furrow using a trowel.

Germinate: When a seed sprouts it has germinated and a baby plant starts to grow.

General-purpose potting compost: There are lots of different types of compost but a general-purpose compost is a good place to begin. This is a special mixture of soil that is good for seedlings and plants.

Half-hardy: A half-hardy plant can die when it gets very cold and frosty and should only be planted outside during the summer.

Hardy: A hardy plant is quite tough and can live outside all year round as it will not be damaged by frost.

Harvest: When the crops that you have grown are ready to be picked, you harvest them by picking or cutting them. The harvest shows that it is the end of the growing cycle for that crop.

Manure: Animal manure is often a mix of animal poo and bedding straw. Gardeners always advise you to use 'well-rotted' manure as this is better for the plants and doesn't smell! 'Well-rotted' means that it has been left to rot for a little while. You can do this yourself by leaving it in a heap in your garden for at least 6 months before you dig it into the soil.

Nutrient: Something that plants and people need to live and grow.

Onion set: A small onion bulb.

Organic: Organic farming recognizes the direct connection between our health and the food we eat. Strict regulations, known as 'standards', define what organic farmers can and cannot do and focus on the protection of wildlife and the environment. Fruit and vegetables that have been grown without the use of harmful chemicals to kill off pests and weeds are called 'organic'.

Perennial: A plant that lives and produces fruits, vegetables or flowers for many years.

Plug plant: A little plant grown from a seed in a small pot of compost and that can be taken out of its pot and 'plugged' straight into your garden or bigger pot to keep growing.

Prune: Sometimes plants need to be cut (pruned) back, but you will need to ask an adult to do this.

Repot: To move a plant from one pot to a bigger pot so that it has more room to grow.

Runner: A long stem that grows roots at the tip to make a new plant. The mother plant shoots runners and these then grow into baby plants.

Seedling: A baby plant that has grown from a seed.

Thinning: Pulling out weak, small seedlings to make room for the others to grow big and strong. You can often eat the seedlings, for example very small carrots can still be delicious mixed into a salad.

Tilth: An area of land that is prepared for sowing and then seeds are sown and crops are grown there.

Tuber: The swollen part of the stem or root that grows underground. Potatoes are called tubers.

Water butt: To help recycle rain water, catch the rain in a big plastic container called a water butt. You can then use this water to water your plants. This helps to reduce the amount of water that you use, so you are helping the environment, and your plants prefer drinking rain water to tap water.

Waterlogged: When the soil is too wet and heavy, plants will be unable to grow beause of a lack of oxygen and life in the soil.

COOKING

Blanching: When you plunge a vegetable like green beans into boiling water very quickly and then take it out and put it straight into cold water to cool down. (You will need an adult to help you do this.)

Bring to a simmer: This is when you bring water up to just below boiling point – you will see small bubbles on the surface.

Bring to the boil: When you bring water to the boil, for pasta for example, the liquid will be really bubbling.

Fold in: You will often need to do this when you are baking cakes. Using a metal spoon, gradually fold the flour into the creamed butter and sugar mixture. Move the spoon in a figure-of-eight movement. Do this gently so that you keep the air in the mixture instead of beating it all out.

Pestle and mortar: A pestle is a heavy stick with one slightly bigger round end and a mortar is a bowl. Both the pestle and mortar are normally made of hard wood, clay, marble or stone. A pestle and mortar are used to crush, grind or mix ingredients together by bashing the ingredients with the pestle in the mortar.

stockists & suppliers

B&Q
Tel: 0845 609 6688
www.diy.com
Check online for your nearest store.
Wide selection of terracotta plant pots
and saucers, gardening tools, plants
and seeds for fruit, vegetables and
edible flowers.

BARCOMBE NURSERIES
Mill Lane
Barcombe
Lewes
East Sussex BN8 5TH
Tel: 01273 400 011
Organic nursery north of Lewes.

BLOOMING MARVELLOUS
Tel: 0845 458 7408
www.bloomingmarvellous.co.uk
Cute outdoor clothing and wellington
boots for the youngest little gardeners.

CAPITAL GARDENS
www.capitalgardens.co.uk
Great selection of plants and seeds, plus a
variety of cute kid-sized tools, gloves,
rain capes, Wellington boots, and garden
baskets and trugs in both traditional
styles and fun bright colours.

CHELSEA GARDENER
125 Sydney Street
King's Road
London SW3 6NR
Tel: 020 7352 5656
www.chelseagardener.com
Supplier of plants, seeds, pots, containers
and other gardening essentials.

CLIFTON NURSERIES
5A Clifton Villas
London W9 2PH
Tel: 020 7289 6851
www.clifton.co.uk
Gardening haven in central London:
plants, pots and gardening essentials.

COOLINGS GARDEN CENTRE
Rushmore Hill
Knockholt
Kent TN14 7NN
Tel: 0800 612 2643
www.coolings.co.uk
Gardening centre in Kent supplying
seeds, compost, tools, pots and more.

FLINT
49 High Street
Lewes
East Sussex BN7 2DD
Tel: 01273 474166
www.flintcollection.com
Beautiful homewares, some of which are
featured in this book.

GARDENER & COOK
www.gardenerandcookstores.co.uk
With two shops and a website, Gardener
& Cook stocks many good-quality
utensils for the garden and the kitchen.

GREAT LITTLE TRADING CO.
Tel: 0844 848 6000
www.gltc.co.uk
Online suppliers of all things child-
related with a range of children's aprons,
cute bakeware and children's gardening
tools and junior planting kits.

HABITAT
196–199 Tottenham Court Road
London W1T 7PJ
Tel: 0844 499 4686
www.habitat.co.uk
Beautiful plant pots and occasional
cooking and gardening accessories
for children.

HOMEBASE
www.homebase.co.uk
Check online for your nearest store.
They sell packet seeds, plant pots,
planters, hanging baskets, seed trays,
gardening labels and more. Children's
gardening tools are available seasonally.

IKEA
www.ikea.com
Check online to order a catalogue or for
your nearest store. Seasonal selection of
gardening furniture and plant pots, plus
miniature cookware for children.

JEKKA'S HERB FARM
Rose Cottage, Shellards Lane
Alveston
Bristol BS35 3SY
01454 418878
www.jekkasherbfarm.com
A specialist all-organic herb nursery.

JOHN LEWIS
Tel: 08456 049 049
www.johnlewis.com
Check online for your nearest store.
Good seasonal selection of tools,
watering cans and seeds for young
gardeners as well as children's bakeware.

LAKELAND
Tel: 01539 488 100
www.lakeland.co.uk
Specialists in everything you might need
in the kitchen, with a good range of
child-friendly equipment including
aprons, bakeware sets and more.

THE LAURELS
171–172 High Street
Lewes
East Sussex BN7 1YE
Tel: 01273 470 248
www.thelaurelsonline.co.uk
Suppliers of some of the beautiful oil
cloth and fabric featured in this book.

LETTERBOX
Tel: 0844 557 5263
www.letterbox.co.uk
All sorts of children's toys, creative
projects and educational fun, including
gardening tools for younger children and
cooking sets for budding little chefs.

LIVE LIKE THIS
74 High Street
Cowes
Isle of Wight PO31 7AJ
Tel: 01983 299559
www.livelikethis.co.uk
Suppliers of some of the beautiful oil
cloth featured in this book.

RICE
www.rice.dk
Kitchenware and homeware in bright
colours, including paper cupcake cases
that children will love.

STEAMER TRADING
Tel: 01273 403 000
www.mycookshop.com
Sussex cookshops and online supplier
of quality cookware.

SUTTONS
Tel: 0844 922 0606
www.suttons.co.uk
Flower and vegetable seeds, as
well as a special selection of child-
friendly seeds that will appeal to kids and
are easy to grow.

THORNBACK & PEEL
Studio W11
Cockpit Arts
Cockpit Yard
Northington Street
London WC1N 2NP
Tel: 020 7242 7478
www.thornbackandpeel.co.uk
Printed textiles as featured in this book.

WICKLE
24 High Street
Lewes
East Sussex BN7 2LU
Tel: 01273 487969
www.wickle.co.uk
Desirable homeware.

**WYEVALE GARDEN
CENTRES**
www.wyevale.co.uk
Check online for your nearest store.
Plants, seeds and gardening tools,
including a mini range especially
for children.

index

acknowledgements

Thanks to my three for helping Daddy to make the raised beds and for continuing to show me how exciting it is for children to learn how to grow and cook their own food.

Thanks to Vicki and Alison for believing in me and my ideas. Thank you once again Tara and Iona – phew, we did it! Tara, the photos are gorgeous, as always. Iona, your endless lists paid off and the book is clear and easy to follow, as well as looking beautiful – hurrah and well done! Thanks Céline for being so fantastically scrupulous and for your calm and reassuring voice at the end of the phone.

Thanks too to Leslie and the rest of the team at Ryland Peters and Small. Thanks Jess for helping to find some lovely children and for introducing me to Julia and her beautiful garden. Thank you, Julia, for the use of your wonderful garden.

Thanks to Louise from **Barcombe Nurseries**, East Sussex, for all your invaluable knowledge about growing fruits and vegetables.

The publisher would like to thank the lovely models who appear in this book:

Ella, Lola & Finley; Liliana & Saskia; Annabel & Thomas; Noah & Gabriel; Alexandra & Kirsty; Lotti; Archie; Ishbel; Max; Huwaida & Ilaina; Joseph & Daniel; Maxi & Lenka; & Roman.

Thank you to the following shops for some of the wonderful props pictured in this book (see pages 124–5 for complete contact details):

Wickle www.wickle.co.uk

Flint www.flintcollection.com

Live Like This www.livelikethis.co.uk

The vegetable garden featured on pages 1, 2, 3, 5l, r, 13al, ar, br, 14–17, 18l,c, 20, 24, 32, 33ac, bl, 34bl, br, 37a, b, 38–39, 40–41, 57al, br, 59, 62, 64al, br, 65a, 80–81, 83, 84c, b, 85, 86–87, 89, 100, 101al, ar, br, 104, 105a, b, 107a, 113, 123, 124b, 128 (key: a=above, b=below, r=right, l=left, c=centre) is Christopher Fields in Sussex, where various vegetable garden courses are available with the owner, Julia Parker. For further information, email julia@parker.gb.com

BW 01/01